بِسْمِ ٱللَّهِ ٱلرَّحْمَٰنِ ٱلرَّحِيمِ

In the name of Allāh
Most Compassionate
Ever Merciful

EARLY FEEDBACK FROM THE #HIFDH COMMUNITY

"It is filled with a lot of good tips and observations that will surely benefit many!"

"I am very happy that you have created such a very important book."

"..the book was amazing.. reading it felt as though you had written some of my own experiences for me.. especially regarding the many different teachers and their manners of teaching and so on.. it took me many years to finish just 13 ajzaa.. yet last year alone I completed the remainder 17"

"Qari has inspired me on so many levels and moved me to act"

"I must say, Masha'Allah, it is beautifully written. Inspiring all others like me who are desperate for motivation."

"I don't know where I would be without Qari at the moment."

Go check it out here (it's free):
http://www.howtomemorisethequran.com/25-methods

I'll see you on the inside!

Qāri Mubashir Anwar

ISBN-10: 1517246040
ISBN-13: 978-1517246044

The
Promise
of Ten

HOW AN *ORDINARY* PERSON
CAN MEMORISE THE QUR'ĀN
IN 6 MONTHS

QARI MUBASHIR ANWAR

To my guides, my mother and father

To my teachers around the world

How to Memorise the Qur'an

Actionable Methods & Advice For All

*"Let the beauty of what you love
be what you do."*

- MAWLANA JALAL AL-DIN AL-RŪMI

*"Ask yourself what makes you come
alive and then go do that.
Because what the world needs
is people who have come alive."*

- HOWARD THURMAN

CONTENTS

HALF WAY DONE BUT IT'S TIME TO LEAVE

TIME FOR A FRESH START

TRICKY TIMES

COMPLETION

THE JOURNEY BEGINS NOW

INTRODUCTION

I can't remember the exact date I started to memorise the Qur'ān.

What I can say, for sure, is that I was around 11 to 13 years old at the time. It was around this point in my life where my connection towards the Qur'ān began to grow. At the time, I was attending a class at a local mosque. I'd never been to a mosque class before, I was used to going to read at an old lady's house - may Allāh bless her. Under her guidance, I'd already read at least two complete readings of the Qur'ān, memorised a few chapters, various other prayers and even learnt the Urdu language. Every day we had to read some Qur'ān, memorise, memorise more and do some language. It was intense but, whatever she did worked.

When my father learnt about the opening of a new mosque close by, he decided to enrol me and my younger brother into the Qur'ān classes. It was a big change. We were used to going down the road to a house. The mosque was a little further but we only used to read some Qur'ān and return home two hours later.

Things changed fast.

I began to be asked again and again if I wanted to start a journey to memorise the Qur'ān. So I took the leap and got started. Everything that has followed came as a result of that day. That leap of faith took me to experience different contexts, cultures and continents.

Since then I've immersed myself in 'trying' to memorise the Qur'ān, learning the sciences of the Qur'ān and the Dīn whilst increasing my interest and involvement in education and community initiatives.

I believe that where you start in life shouldn't dictate where you finish in it. No tool can more profoundly unlock a person's ability to change his or her place in life than access to quality education. The good news is that we have the ability to provide quality education to every child on earth right now. I've been teaching children and adults for free for around a decade now, and will continue to do so as long as I am able to.

I believe there's a lot to do within the field. Our children are not only the future but, they are the now. What we do today shapes the world. Throughout the years, I've seen and experienced different issues facing the Muslim community. The topmost has been education. However no individual can solve these problems alone. A collective effort is needed, and we each have a unique role to play. I'm not going to talk about this though. This book will explore everything that has led to this point in my life.

***

This is a story about what happens when you recognise that there's more in this world for you to become. That you don't have to have certain things to make contributions to the world. It's a story about a journey from doubt to conviction. The story of my journey so far, but it's a story that can belong to anyone.

The book briefly takes you through how I began my journey to memorise the Qur'ān. What happened, what I did and all I had to go through. My hope is that it reflects what an ordinary journey I've had, and one that speaks to many of you. I hope it also demonstrates exactly what goes into memorisation. I don't think people realise the amount of work people put into memorisation.

When writing this book, I wanted to have thirty chapters like the divisional structure of the Qur'ān. But I didn't manage to do that. Maybe I'll add a couple more chapters in a later edition. I intended that each chapter be titled with a principle. Each principle having been lessons I'd learnt during my journey. The principles serve as guides and I believe they are great truths. I used them for both small and major decisions I had to make. I hope they will be carried forward, shared with others, and adopted in ways that will help you on your own journey. Not only for memorisation but in life too. The book is not only relevant to Ḥifẓ but life too.

The single thing that allows one to live his or her dreams is converting a spark of inspiration into immediate action. We have to take small steps, then chase the footprints you'll want to leave behind. I hope this book helps you find yours because "what you seek is seeking you." - Rūmi

Qārī Mubashir Anwar

GETTING
STARTED

BIG DREAMS START WITH SMALL ACTS

"Great things are done by a series of small things brought together."
— Vincent Van Gogh

***

Growing up I used to listen to the Qur'ān during journeys in the car.

Only my dad would know why he used to play the tapes but maybe it had something to do with me and my siblings. I picked up things from hearing the audio each day. I memorised verses and imitated the reciters. I picked up melody and most importantly an inclination towards reading with the correct

Makhārij. Makhārij is the plural of the word Makhraj - meaning the place where a letter of the Arabic language is pronounced from. This became natural to me.

But memorising the Qur'ān wasn't natural to me. It wasn't something that I'd chosen to do. It wasn't a big dream that I had as a child.

It was my father's dream. He wished that one of us (the boys of the house) memorised. Not sure about the girls! He'd tell me "I tried with your elder brother, but he refused. He didn't want to read to anyone after his teacher passed away. So you and your younger brother are my only hope now."

So there it was. The sparks of the beginning began to appear. My father would talk to me about memorising, he'd tell me about its rewards, and encourage me to go for it. I'm pretty sure the first time I heard the Ḥadīth about the one who memorised the Qur'ān could take with them ten people to paradise, was from my father.

This was where the 'Promise of Ten' came about.

I just said what I always said, 'I don't know'. You can ask my family this was a typical response from me to questions. All I knew was that my father had this dream and I was potentially the one to make it happen. So I thought 'Why not, I'll have a go and we'll see what happens.'

When I'd finished my third or fourth complete reading of the Qur'ān, these discussions were taking place. My father would speak to my teacher about it all the time. It was all new to me but I was excited. The teacher was encouraging too with frequent praise and votes of confidence. That helped with motivation.

What motivated me even more were the things I found to be amazing.

It was amazing that my teacher's entire family had all memorised the Qur'ān. All the brothers and sisters were Ḥuffāẓ. This was the case in each generation of the family. In this sense they were all people of the Qur'ān. Even today this tradition is still going strong within the family. I've never seen such attention from a family towards the preservation and recitation of the Qur'ān. At the same time though, I couldn't help but think about how many of them may have felt 'compelled' to do it: 'Imagine I am the first guy who doesn't do it'. I knew there was pressure on some of them because the new generation of the family were memorising in my class. We were classmates.

For me it was different, no one in the family was a Ḥāfiẓ and like most families, we didn't have such strong connection with the Qur'ān. It was fascinating to learn though that there were Ḥuffāẓ in my family tree. The chance for me to be the next in line was an exciting prospect.

Before I knew it I had started memorising.

I began from the 30th Juz, Sūrah al-Nās and worked my way up to Sūrah al-Naba'. Having memorised a lot of the Suwar under my former teacher - the elderly lady. I remember feeling good about things on the first day because I'd memorised a quarter of the Juz already. I felt I could do this and do it quickly.

***

At the time, there was a lot happening. The daily routines were: school, mosque, homework, school, mosque, homework (and exams). In the middle of all this, things began to change drastically the moment I heard the following words being recited:

"Surely, there has passed over man a period of time when he was not a thing worth mentioning. Surely, We created man from a fertilized ovum that We keep turning and examining (from one stage to the next till birth). So We have made him (in the order of) hearing (then) seeing. Indeed, We

also showed him the way (to understanding and insight for distinguishing between the truth and falsehood) whether he (now) becomes thankful or continues to be ungrateful."
— Sūrah al-Insān (76:1-4)

And then...

"By the (endless expanse and infinite space of) heaven and the Nightly (discernable) Visitant. And what do you know what the Nightly (discernable) Visitant is? (It implies) every heavenly body (be it a star, a planet, or any of the heavenly spheres) which shines and brightens (the space). There is no human soul but with a protector (appointed) over it."
— Sūrah at-Ṭāriq (86:1-4)

It was a tape cassette in my uncle's office.

I was alone in the room. Being a nosey kid, thinking I was Sherlock Holmes perhaps. After finding the tape, I was curious to know what was on it so I played it. What I heard that day changed my life.

It was a unique sound but astonishingly strange. I remember asking myself "Who is this? Why does he read so slow? Why does he read so strange? Why does he read low, deep and then so high pitched? Why?" I had to find out who this guy on the tape was. This must have been in 1999 or there about. Google was different then, it was still in beta. I can't remember if I Googled him or not, but I did go straight to my uncle and dad. It turned out to be someone who had passed away when I was just one years old. He was known as a legend, the voice of Makkah, the voice of angels. None other than the iconic Shaykh al-Qārī 'Abdul Bāsiṭ 'Abdus Samad - May Allāh elevate and bless his soul. (Watch YouTube video, named "Abdul Basit Abdul Samad : The Voice of Mecca for a short bio).

This small incident changed my life. He became role-model-like for me and my daily hobby during high school (and college). I gained a greater purpose to become a reciter and it gave my memorisation a lot more joy. Recitation became as Rūmi described that "when you do things from your soul, you feel a river moving in you, a joy."

Suddenly I wasn't only memorising anymore, even my teacher noticed I began to recite differently. So he asked me to become the reciter at a weekly assembly. I started doing what he called "Mashq" exercises - he would recite, and I would follow. But because I used to listen to 'Abdul Bāsiṭ I wanted to do things differently. So each time my teacher would recite, I'd add something else to it much to his surprise, when in fact I was supposed to be imitating him. We soon stopped doing it. He asked me to start reading in public instead. I was ready.

I started on the 27th night of Ramaḍān - I remember wearing my red hat, blue fleece top and white thobe. Terrified. Eyes closed. In the back of my mind that tape cassette was playing. I started reciting Sūrah at-Ṭāriq exactly as I'd first heard it on that tape cassette. The rest is as they say was 'history'.

***

Soon it wasn't only me memorising in the family, my little brother followed, my cousins and some of my friends. Even relatives, their friends, and friends of friends got inspired to memorise after seeing me memorise and recite in public. Some of them are now Ḥāfiẓ, some even completed it before I did, but most didn't manage to do the whole thing. My dad used to say to not shy away from public recitals because doing go would inspire others. He was right.

No one saw any of this coming.

It goes to show that the smallest of things can lead to greater things. They can change directions. My time with the Qur'ān changed me. For the first time, I began to fully understand that there was a great vastness to the Qur'ān. It was much more than memorisation. It was an incredible oral phenomena.

I started to think about what it would be like if this mosque hadn't been opened. If I hadn't had the urge to pick up that cassette and listen to what was on it, or if my father hadn't told me about his desires and dreams. I'd always been someone who liked to be different and not follow the norms of peers. I knew I was different but ordinary. There's nothing special about me, it is the Qur'ān that makes the ordinary extraordinary. I wasn't in my comfort zone that's for sure. This was something new. True self-discovery only begins when you bring an end to your comfort zone, and mine was about to end far more quickly than I'd anticipated.

CONCENTRATE ON THE BIGGER PICTURE

*"Sincerity [Ikhlās] is the believer's plot of land
while his deeds [a'māl] are its surrounding walls.
The walls are subject to alteration and change, but
not so the ground. Only upon dutiful devotion [taqwa]
can a building be firmly based."*

— Shaykh 'Abd al-Qādir al-Jīlāni
(May Allāh be well pleased with him).

***

Although I never made a conscious choice to memorise the Qur'ān, I knew it was a great thing to do. Who wouldn't?

I knew my father wanted it to happen, I even had some encouragement from relatives too but my focus was probably all over the place. As I mentioned before, I had school, memorisation and homework, but now there was Mujawwad recitation like 'Abdul Bāsiṭ too.

So why was I memorising the Qur'ān?

I used to ask myself this question many times. My dad may have been the key reason. I started because he pushed it. I started because he got me into it though he knew I wanted it more. As I became more self-aware and learnt more I had my own reasons to memorise. It wasn't about my father anymore. It was about me.

When I started, I was told that it would take around three years to complete. This was supposed to be the 'average' and the norm for students in such classes. There was no reason why I couldn't do it too. The key focus then, was time. It isn't surprising that it's the same in many places today. Yes, time is important, time is precious and time is short. It's reasonable to want to finish in a certain time frame before you get busy with adult life. Makes sense right?

I learnt, however, it's more sensible to focus on the bigger picture.

Memorisation was like a race for me at the time. I was competing against classmates and against time. I'd race to finish first and memorise the most. I'd even sometimes compete to be the best reciter even if I never admitted to it. I've always been a perfectionist so I would always concentrate on getting things perfect. So in an attempt to avoid getting told off or hit by the teacher I went crazy on the memorisation. Robot like within classes. But guess what, there was no focus on revision at all. It was all about recitation which is a mistake for anyone memorising.

When you ask people why they're memorising the Qur'ān or why they did so, you usually get typical responses.

- My mum or dad wanted me to do it;
- I did it for Allāh (even though they may not truly have understood what that may mean);
- I wanted to gain the rewards for memorisation like the crown, the promise of ten and other things.

I was in the same camp. My intentions weren't focused enough at the start. It was like I was only doing this for a person. There didn't seem to be any real reason to it. I don't know if you ever had the feeling when you used to go to school and you never wanted to be there. Waking up in the morning and thinking, 'Not school again. Why do I have to go? I can't wait for holidays'. It was a bit like this for me. Don't get me wrong though, I used to love going to the mosque during the first few years. I would race to get there. I'd get dressed straight away at home when back from school. What I'm trying to say is, it felt like it was a must without choice at times.

Pretty much straight away my dad talked to me about intentions. Telling me that you are doing this for the pleasure of Allāh and His Messenger (peace and blessings of Allāh be upon him). We'll talk about this more later.

***

There is a great truth that I have got to mention. We have become too obsessed with 'memorisation'. We have become agitated and impatient for the finishing line. Many parents get carried away with the desire for their children to memorise the Qur'ān. Their thoughts get clouded by the great rewards in the hereafter and much more. Anyone would love to have a crown placed on their head on the Day of Judgment but, there's a bigger picture to think about. Not for our sake but the sake of the memoriser.

There are two types of mindsets you can adopt:

(a) The Memorisation Box Mindset
(b) The Memorisation Journey Mindset

THE MEMORISATION BOX MINDSET

This is looking at memorisation within the context of the Qur'ān. The things mentioned above are some examples. People concentrating on memorisation, the process, technique and completion. A focus on the mechanics but ignoring the dynamics. It's a memorisation race mindset. I had this mindset for so long.

Frankly, it's a battle to move out of it.

You might change your mindset yourself but others around you might not. Your parents or your teachers may still have the same mindset. So you find yourself continually bombarded with questions and statements like:

- "How much have you memorised now?"
- "Why is memorisation taking you so long for?"
- "You should be finishing within x number of years - what's the matter?"
- "You should eat y and z, and recite a and b to boost your

memory."

Things like this came at me all the time. It took something to happen to change my thoughts and we'll mention that in the next chapter.

THE MEMORISATION JOURNEY MINDSET

This is what you need to aim for. This is looking at memorisation in the context of Islām. In the context of Dīn: your transactional life with Allāh. It's looking at memorisation as a journey of life as opposed to a journey to finish memorisation.

It's a shift from saying:

"What is my purpose in becoming a Ḥāfiẓ?" to "What are my objectives for memorising in Islām, Dīn and life?"

Becoming a Ḥāfiẓ is one thing, and memorising the Qur'ān as a Muslim is another. If you make becoming "Ḥāfiẓ" the end-goal of your mission there's nothing wrong with that. It was my mission and it is likely to be or had been yours too. The thing is that it needs more depth. It needs context, it needs a step by step goal orientated journey.

For example, if the purpose were to be a blanket statement: "I want to become a Ḥāfiẓ in x number of days" what happens if you fail? You'll make anew or you'll think you're a failure (or maybe not).

If you said instead, "I'm going to start memorising the Qur'ān because as a Muslim I believe that I have to do such and such a thing. And my first goal is to memorise the 30th chapter which I can then use to do such and such a thing." Like this you're more likely to progress with better focus. You make small goals along the way that slowly build up to the finishing line.

Remember, memorisation is not a race or a marathon but it is a journey for life.

***

So what are some of the objectives of memorising the Qur'ān under this mindset?

1. SEEKING THE ACCEPTANCE AND PLEASURE OF ALLĀH AND HIS PROXIMITY

This is without doubt amongst the most supreme intentions for memorising the Qur'ān. Make this your aim. Remember these are the Words of Allāh. You might tell me you are memorising because of your parents just like I might have. Perhaps instead say, "I seek the pleasure of Allāh by fulfilling my duty to my parents."

You may say I'm memorising because it is a dream of mine to be able to say "I have committed to memory 600+ pages containing the Words of Allāh." You should instead say, "I seek the pleasure and acceptance of Allāh through aiming to protect His Words by Ḥifẓ."

One of the quickest ways to become close to Allāh is to become closer to His Beloved (peace and blessings of Allāh be upon him). One of the prime methods to do that is through the Qur'ān itself. So make proximity part of your mindset.

2. TO IMPROVE YOUR PRAYER AND ENJOY IT

This is a basic thing, but it's something that we've forgotten these days. Many Ḥuffāẓ race to finish reading just like those who haven't memorised. They always read the same verses when leading the prayer on rotate. Why would you memorise the Qur'ān if you are just going to read certain chapters or portions all the time. There might be a genuine reason you'd do it like the Ansāri mentioned in the Ḥadīth of Anas, who used to recite Sūrah Ikhlās in every rak'ah. His reason was his love for the Sūrah because it speaks about Allāh, upon which the Prophet (peace and blessings of Allāh be upon him) said he would enter into Paradise.

But your memorisation should be a means to make your prayer better. You can recite long passages and short, you can recite from different places, or you can recite the whole Qur'ān - why not.

This is something I never appreciated when memorising. My dad always told me to recite the Qur'ān as revision in the daily prayers. He always told me to stop reading the smaller Suwar and recite other verses (when leading the prayer). I didn't do it. Most people don't do it. My reasons for not doing so was in light of those praying behind me. I could easily start reading Sūrah Baqarah but you have to take others into account. There could be people who can't stand for long and others who have to leave. Most people have to realise this through experience. I am no different. Start to recite the Qur'ān as revision in the prayer. Just try it. Reciting in the prayer will make your memorisation stronger.

Remember a lot of people may only know between one to four chapters by heart, if not up to ten. Their prayers are on the same routine all the time. Pencil in your prayers as a goal.

A point related to this, and one that I find annoying is that memorisation has become about leading the Tarawīḥ night prayers in Ramaḍān. As if memorisation is centred around it. I've found this to be the case in certain circles. Again this is all to do with mindset. This is wrong on so many levels. It illustrates one thing – people need to think more long term and adopt a broader mentality.

3. ENJOYING RECITATION

The more you memorise the more you should enjoy it. Visit: http://www.howtomemorisethequran.com/quran-love-letter/ for an interesting but beautiful take on the Qur'ān.

When memorising, you make so much repetition. Through that repetition, you make corrections and through that you improve your recitation. You should make the sweetness and enjoyment of the recitation of the Qur'ān a goal. Memorising with this in your mindset makes listening to the Qur'ān an enjoyment too. Don't underestimate listening.

4. TO INSPIRE ACTION ACCORDING TO THE QUR'ĀN

A Ḥadīth which I've discussed (http://howtomemorisethequran. com/thehigheststationinparadise/) talks about the Sāhib al Qur'ān. As pointed out the word 'Sāhib' can mean companion, friend, holder, keeper, or authority. Although I like to translate it as 'reciter', in the literal sense it is companionship. Here's the Ḥadīth:

'Abdullāh Ibn 'Amr narrates that the Messenger of Allāh (peace and blessings of Allāh be upon him) said:

"It will be said [on the Day of Judgement] to the reciter* of the Qur'ān:
'Recite and be uplifted [in your rank]! And recite in the distinct manner
(Tartīl) as you used to recite in the world. For indeed your rank [in
Paradise] will be according to the last verse you recite.'"

— Al-Tirmiẕī, Ibn Majāh, Ibn Hibbān, Al-Ḥakim, Bayhaqi,
Ibn Abi Shaybah.

A companion holds a sense of friendship, loyalty, and most importantly – a continuum. If we took this Ḥadīth to mean those who memorised the Qur'ān, we can't say so as a fact. Though a companion is likely to have memorised. One thing for certain is the word 'Sāhib'. Memorisation itself is not the most spectacular thing according to this Ḥadīth. It's a means to an end.

Did you know that there are non-Muslims who read and memorise the Qur'ān? What would make you different? – The emphasis on 'practice'.

This is what the Ḥadīth is indicating by the word 'Sāhib'. Some scholars have even said this reciter will only be able to recite those verses he or she had practised. The companions of the Prophet (peace and blessings of Allāh be upon him, and may Allāh be pleased with them) had this mindset. They would memorise something new only until they'd put into implementation what they had memorised. This is why this is a must in the memorisation journey mindset.

5. TO BECOME A GUARDIAN PRESERVER OF THE QUR'ĀN

Islām has always had an incredible oral tradition. Remember that we're looking at goals within the context of Islām. The transmission of Islamic sciences has been through chains of authority. Ḥadīth went through a rigorous transmission process and the principles were then made solid. Likewise, the Qur'ān is impossible to distort due to millions adhering to the same oral tradition.

Imām Muslim quotes from 'Abdu'llāh ibn al-Mubārak, who states: *"The Isnād (chain of authority) is a necessary part of Dīn. If there was no chain of authority then everyone would have said whatever he wanted to say."*

So remembering this, no matter how much you memorise you are contributing to the preservation of the Qur'ān.

6. MEMORISE AS PREPARATION FOR FURTHER STUDIES

Knowing the Qur'ān by heart creates a strong foundation for studying further and makes it easier. There are many traditional schools that make it a prerequisite that you are a Ḥāfiẓ before you can study under them. Many great scholars also had and have the same policy.

Say you don't intend to memorise the whole Qur'ān, you can one day take what you've memorised, understand it, and act upon it. If you wanted to memorise the whole Qur'ān but never made it there – you can use that memorisation to drive further study.

7. TO INCULCATE A LIFE-LONG LOVE AND ENGAGEMENT WITH THE QUR'ĀN

This process should already have begun before you learnt how to read the Qur'ān. We learnt, recited, and completed the Qur'ān in the mosque but then left it. The reason is that there was no engagement. There was no love. Personally, I tend to refuse to teach children aged between 5 to 7 and have managed to do so 99% of the time. I prefer that they play and hear stories from the Qur'ān instead. In this way, they grow up listening to the Qur'ān knowing it as a story or a guide book from God! Following that they immerse themselves into the Arabic textual universe, all excited.

It seems, however, our aims are for children to despise the Qur'ān. We have engineered everything in a way which is void of any fun or meaning. In the context of memorisation, far too often we pressurise ourselves or our children. The pressure is often the race to complete it. Despite wanting good, this results in the opposite.

When you're memorising, you're not doing it for the now but you're going to be doing it for the rest of your life.

Those who find themselves pressurised either (1) quit (2) want to finish immediately or (3) finish and then never come back to it. When you sell a product or service and you do a great job, the customers remember it well but they won't boast about it. If you got on their bad side, they'll want to tell the whole world. Likewise, when you memorise under pressure you remember those days more than the good days.

8. MAKING ENGAGEMENT WITH THE QUR'ĀN EASIER

Engagement with the Qur'ān centres around three things: (1) recitation, (2) study, and (3) reflection.

RECITATION.

Memorising makes recitation easier. As a memoriser or someone who has memorised you are bound to recite more. Revision, prayers, invites, and wherever you may be. A Ḥāfiẓ can make the simple plan of covering the revision via prayer – this is easy to do. You can cover at least a third of the Qur'ān, a whole Qur'ān or two - so why read the last 20 Sūrah all the time?

STUDY / REFLECTION.

Thousands of Ḥuffāẓ do not study the translation of the Qur'ān (if they have no understanding) even once ever.

After an amazing effort, they've done nothing. You have ample opportunity to do so. An opportunity far greater than those who haven't memorised. Studying and reflecting over the Qur'ān is for all mankind. Not just for scholars. Yes, perhaps there are a small number of verses to do with law that scholars attention is most needed, but the Qur'ān is for us all to think over. Allāh commands so. We just leave matters of derivative jurisprudence to the inheritors of the Prophet (peace and blessings be upon him). Thinking along in these three stages will improve your memorisation journey.

The importance of Arabic cannot be underestimated. Most of us memorise without understanding. It's important to either learn the language first, during or after memorisation. Your engagement, intellect, memory, and sharpness will increase.

9. MAKING A LIFE-LONG COMMITMENT TO STUDYING ISLAMIC KNOWLEDGE

If a child or adult has memorised the Qur'ān, they've proven something: they can memorise, they are good at it. That means you can memorise anything else like the core texts of the Qur'ān. So make it a goal when you memorise looking ahead whether that be texts of Tajwīd or Ḥadīth.

10. GAIN THE VIRTUES OF THE QUR'ĀN

You read and hear about many virtues from the salvation of the self and family members to the company of the elite angels and prophets. Notice that practice comes first, followed by virtue. Many of us make the rewards or virtues our sole goal. It should be within the mindset but in the end. The reason to include it in your mindset is that it allows you to contemplate over the hereafter and the rewards therein. It's good motivation too!

***

Going back to my story, I only just started memorising so my mindset was still developing. As an ordinary young guy, you can forgive me for looking at memorisation as a race. You can forgive me for putting emphasis on recitation. But it's better that you realise this is not the right way to go about it as soon as possible. My realisation was just around the corner.

RECOGNISE & REMEMBER THAT YOU HAVE A PURPOSE

"Actions are valued according to the intentions, and every man is credited with what he intended. If someone's emigration was to Allāh and His Messenger (peace and blessings of Allāh be upon him), his emigration was thus to Allāh and His Messenger (peace and blessings of Allāh be upon him). And if someone's emigration was to get a worldly benefit or to take a woman in marriage, his emigration was to that which he emigrated."

— The Beloved of Allāh, our master Muḥammad (peace and blessings of Allāh be upon him) as narrated by 'Umar b. Al-Khaṭṭāb (may Allāh be well pleased with him).

***

Soon my teacher started calling me "Ḥāfiẓ Jinn." Bizarre hey?

He claimed that when I am to be all grown up many people will come to know me and begin listening to me. "You will be like a mighty Jinn," he claimed. Since that day I've been reciting in public so that's around 17-18 years (at the time of writing). As strange as it may sound I've always been a cautious, quiet and shy kind of guy. Thinking a lot on the inside. Keeping things to myself. Not trusting many people. It's one of the reasons I prefer to write, but few would argue that I've changed despite speaking/performing in public. I even get requests for making YouTube channels which is worse.

When I was memorising I came to understand that I was gifted with recitation. My dad would tell me that I've been given my voice and abilities for a reason - you have to go out and bring people to Islām through it. So I should regularly practise. I never did to be honest. I was getting calls to recite on TV, events and to make CD recordings. I refused to do everything and anything other than mosque events. How could I start doing all of this when I'm still memorising, but why would I at all?

I used to read many books on spirituality and I understood many concepts. I thought it could corrupt my intentions, distract me, remember small things can lead to big changes. It could have shifted my attentions away from memorisation. I didn't want any attention though. I like to be at the back-end. So I kept things local. I kept things focused.

Even then though, I still wasn't there yet with the bigger picture.

My typical daily routine looked something like this:

- Get up at around 8am and go to school.
- Come back at around 3:30pm.
- Have something to eat maybe whilst watching some TV (most likely cartoons).
- Rush out to go to the mosque at 4:30pm.
- Memorise in the mosque for 2 hours: new lesson and previous lessons.
- Come back home, maybe play games on Playstation or outside.
- Eat dinner.
- Do school work or play games maybe.
- Go to sleep.

As you can see memorisation was only memorisation at the mosque. This was the case with many people. It's often the only time for Qur'ān nowadays too.

This was just the start of my journey. I'd say there are five phases in my pursuit to memorising the Qur'ān and beyond. Being at this first mosque is phase one.

I started memorising from the 30th Juz and it might have taken me a few months to memorise. After that I went onto the 1st Juz. At times, I memorised whatever section I was tasked with, otherwise I would memorise all I could cram in within two hours. At the start I used to memorise a few lines. I'd repeat words and combine them. We used to memorise very little a day.

It took me a while to get through Sūrah al-Baqarah. I know of stories where people memorised it within a month, more or less. For me it felt like I'd come to the Sūrah that was going to put me to my first real test. And so it was. It felt like it was going to take me years getting past it. Everyone memorising will and has to come across a Sūrah or a portion that will give them a real test.

I was in high school (UK 11-16 age range) when I started memorising, specifically when I was in year 7 or 8. As a student, there was pressure on me from home, school, and mosque. So it wasn't easy. I used to memorise only a few lines and would hardly revise.

Another big issue was that the teachers began to change. Teachers came in and out of the mosque. This didn't help with consistency and momentum. If you think that was a problem, there were more to come. I used to get ill every two weeks taking another week or so off memorisation. It was typically blamed on the evil eye due to my public recitals. When school exams came up, I'd take further days off. So my journey from the very beginning was testing.

Clearly it was becoming a tough journey for consistency, but along came an incident that would change things again. Something that left a mark forever.

***

My primary school friend and neighbour began to attend my classes with me to memorise the Qur'ān.

I was part of the reason he began. We used to have races in class to see who would beat each other to finish a certain Sūrah. We'd compete with melodies too, he was always hilarious in everything he came up with. We were kids. Sūrah al-Fajr, the last couple of verses and a random melody. That's what he did. I still remember it exactly today. Sūrah al-Shams - my little brother reminded me the other day - he made a melody for that too. Even he can remember it. May Allāh forgive him (and us) for our errors and raise his ranks.

We used to play sports too. He was an intelligent, creative, artistic and an athletic guy. He was a quick cricket bowler and good with the bat too. We used to go to the same primary school but when we were memorising we were in different schools. He made it to Grammar school whilst I was at the high school in the same area.

Not too long into his journey, he wasn't attending class all the time and he eventually stopped coming. So I hear he got a knee injury in a football game. I remember walking down the streets with him on his clutches. He told me about the game and what happened. Maybe we were coming back from the mosque - I can't remember but it wasn't on our street.

I was under the impression he would come back pretty soon. I remember telling him to drop playing so much and keep focused on what matters. I gave him my example, I never did any activities outside school in order to memorise. It takes sacrifice.

He didn't show any signs of getting better though. This went on for weeks, and I began wondering what happened. I soon found out that he actually had cancer. When I spoke to him, he told me that the knee injury caught an infection and it led to cancer. So one day whilst I'm walking down my street (did I say we lived on the same street?), I see his mum outside and my friend joined her. He was still on crutches but what I saw was shocking. I can still picture it today. His appearance had changed. He was extremely fragile, his skin had darkened markedly, and he'd lost all of his hair. He saw me and smiled. I think we exchanged Salaam, I don't remember much else other than his mum asking me to make a prayer for him.

It was clear he was suffering. I so badly wanted to go and visit him during his time at the hospital. I wasn't allowed to go though due to school GCSE exams.

It wasn't until the day I was revising for a school exam that it all sunk in.

I was sitting at my desk, it was a bright day and I'm suddenly told he'd died. [Speechless]. I couldn't do anything but say 'Surely to Allāh we belong and to Him we shall return.'

The cancer had spread throughout his body and it was too late. Sadly I never made it to his funeral, I never saw him since the day I met him outside his house on his crutches. Again I wasn't allowed to go due to school.

But the truth is that he had never stopped his pursuit for memorisation despite his absence from the mosque. Despite his illness he was still seeking, despite being on deathbed, he was still at it. When I went to visit the family after he passed away, his dad spoke to me about what he got up to. He'd tell me how he never gave up on memorising, at the hospital he would always be reading, and make mention of me and his other friends. In fact, he always had a desire to die with the Qur'ān and in Ramaḍān. That wish came true. We were both 15, but he passed away. It was in November 2002 (Ramaḍān, the days of forgiveness).

This changed everything.

I now recognised and remembered we all have a purpose in life. Time is against us. Out of loss, we gain clarity. When he left us, something deep within me fought back. Why was it that he left? Why was it him and not me? Clearly I was here for a reason. I remember going back to the mosque from that day on reading with a sense of doing things right.

If you want to memorise the Qur'ān - what's stopping you? There are people who are blind, impaired, or facing death doing it.

The Qur'ān and the walking Qur'ān (peace and blessings of Allāh be upon him) are our means to the Creator. Our ultimate purpose. But in reaching that purpose we also have our duties to earth, its inhabitants and its future. I started thinking ahead of what might be in 10, 20, 30 years. Recognising you have a purpose and remembering why you are memorising will be important. Keep the intentions for Allāh and His Messenger (peace and blessings be upon him).

For me, the initiation of the bigger picture only just began.

ALWAYS LOOK FOR BALANCE

"If we can't establish the balance in ourselves,
we can't establish it out there."

— Shaykh Ḥamza Yūsuf

***

By now I'd done around 5 or 6 Juz by heart.

As time frame was always in my mind, I gave a lot of attention to finding a technique that allowed me to learn as much as possible in a small time frame. The goal: become a Ḥāfiẓ before finishing school or college.

There were two things to this: (a) the amount I memorised in two hours and (b) the technique used to do it.

When I started memorising with the 30th Juz I used to memorise single chapters first and then repeat a part of a verse and combine words. This was fairly easy due to them being a couple of lines long, so when I got to chapters that were a page or two pages long, I had to divide them. I'd memorise a couple of lines or verses.

From the combination of words I moved to repeating a verse many times by looking, then without looking, then do the same for the next verse. I would then combine both verses. Move on to the next, combine the three and so on and so forth. I tried to repeat a whole page in one go too. I'd recite the entire page many times, then try to read it from memory. If I couldn't do it all, I'd start from the point I was struggling from.

When I got to the 1st Juz things really slowed down. I don't have access to my green 16-lined Mus'ḥaf (copy of the Qur'ān) I used at the time. It wasn't a Mus'ḥaf I used by choice, it was given to me as a gift to use. Note it's really important that you memorise using one Mus'ḥaf and remain with it. Choose something that is not small but large enough. 15 lines are generally best. It is said that yellowish/brown paper aids the memory. If I had access to it I could have told you how much I was memorising because the amounts were marked. I can say for sure, there were times where I'd be memorising 1, 2 or 3 lines out of the 16. There was no consistency with the amount, but there was consistency in memorisation.

I didn't stop there.

I was looking for ways to boost my memory and the best ways to keep what I'd memorised. I always eat a bunch of almonds every day since then. One of the many habits I developed during those early days. My parents would tell me to have them because they were good for the brain. Particularly, if you soaked them overnight in water and had them in the morning with the skin peeled off.

I'd learn about things to read for memory improvement. I remember reading up about one during my time at the mosque. I wrote it down at the back of the Qur'ān to keep it in mind and showed it to my cousin. It was that whoever recited the first four verses, the verse of the Throne (Ayat-al-Kursi) with the two following verses, and the last three verses of Sūrah al-Baqarah, every night, would never forget the Qur'ān. Whether that works or not is another discussion. Since then, I've learnt of many things and ways to improve memory.

***

The technique you adopt to memorise is dependent on a few things. You will have to ask yourself about:

a. Choosing one copy of the Qur'ān you are comfortable with and sticking to it.

b. How much do you want to learn?

c. How much can you realistically memorise for you to be able to claim "I know this with perfection"? (Remember the aim is not how much you memorise but it's perfection and internalisation of the words).

d. What is your goal? Time-wise when are you aiming for completion?

e. How much time do you have to commit? Can you memorise 2/3 pages a day to reach a goal of 6 months completion? If so how much time do you have in a day?

f. The way you make repetition.

One of the problems I had was that we hardly had any guidance from the teachers. No one spoke to us about these things. Every teacher would just come, take a seat, wait, shout, slap, smack and laugh. They never spoke to students one-on-one on a level to try and figure out how they could improve; nor provide guidance and ideas. I did and had to figure things out myself.

I've never had spectacular memory abilities, but I constantly revised my technique until I reached a method that worked best and continued to develop that. Something I was most comfortable with. Whether I was memorising a few verses or a page. I didn't want to be the norm. I chose to be different, and in doing so, I proved that through struggle personal transformation is possible.

The key thing I got out of this was that you need to find your rhythm as quick as you can. But most crucially, always look for balance.

What is balance in technique?

Balance is getting to a point where you can memorise enough but strongly without any extreme amount of work. No - I'm not saying take the lazy route! I'm saying memorise using all your strengths as opposed to focusing on your weaknesses. Instead of saying, "I can't memorise, I have weak memory - how can

I boost it?" Ask instead, "I know I can memorise but what is it that's working for me? - How can I maximise on that thing that's working?" You don't want to go all out guns blazing. You can see I never did that and it was a gradual process. The Qur'ān teaches us all about processes.

Balance is working with yourself and not against yourself. Balance is avoiding one extreme to another. Balance is the way of our beloved Prophet (peace and blessings of Allāh be upon him) and his community.

This means you don't consider balance just for your memorisation task. When seeking balance in Ḥifẓ, you need to consider your own growth too. Don't forsake other important things like taking care of yourself (wellbeing, health, character) and your family for memorisation.

With anything you do, seek balance.

TIME TO UP
MY GAME

RECITATION EVERY DAY KEEPS THE MEMORY IN STAY

"Jibrīl used to revise the Qur'ān with me once every year, but this year he has revised it with me twice."

— The Messenger of Allāh
(peace and blessings of Allāh be upon him)

***

When I'd memorised around 5 Juz, I decided it was time to leave the mosque.

I left and joined a new one in the area. I had to leave. I'd had enough. The latest teacher to have been employed, although was an amazing Ḥāfiẓ, wasn't so amazing in class. I saw everything:

fights, shouts, blood (yes students bleeding!), tears and runs (think Tom and Jerry!). I didn't want to see it. The original motivation and atmosphere was no longer there. So I decided to leave. We all left, me, my brother and cousins.

Joining a new mosque was exciting. I went to visit them. It was huge. It was much bigger than the first one. They even had a gym there. It was promising. The teacher also spoke English to a decent level. So we had a chat with the parents about moving there, and we did. We got the relatives to invade the mosque too.

When I joined them we all had a rigorous test. I can't remember how bad I did but it was bad. I remember the others being the same. The chapters we memorised at the previous mosque were not strong enough. Although I could read from certain Juz when randomly prompted, I couldn't do the same for the most recent Juz I had memorised. The teacher there said that if one had more than three mistakes in a Juz or section then they didn't know it well enough. The standards were high but I liked that.

The memorisation procedure we were to follow was based on a three-way system used in the sub-continent:

1. The new lesson/memorisation (known as the 'Sabak')
2. The previous day's/weeks lesson(s) (known as the 'Sabki')

3. Revision (known as the Manzil, in other circles called Dor/ Murāja'ah).

We had to recite all three things on a daily basis within two hours. You can imagine, it's difficult.

We came back from a long day at school. Then went to the mosque and we're expected to memorise anywhere between half a page or a page with other kids shouting their heads off. At most times it would take up to two hours to learn the new lesson, forget about revision. At other times, memorising was easy but revision was difficult. This is one of the downsides of the system due to the time we had. The time available wasn't enough. This certainly contributed to why things were going slow and why my revision was being compromised. In my experience, people should spend at least 4 hours for memorisation including revision every day.

My track record of falling ill never stopped either or taking days off for school work. What I'd learnt was that you need to read every day, no matter what. The teachers always repeated this too. Otherwise, you can forget something. You have to repeat continuously up to the point that it's firmly within your long term memory (spaced repetition). Just like you're able to recite Sūrah Fātiha as if it's natural. Even then though, you still need to repeat things. You will God willing, reach a point where what you've memorised will become natural to you but you have to be patient.

At the time of writing I oversee around six young ones for memorisation. Two of them are in high school, the rest of them are in primary school with a great chance to memorise. I see the same issues with them and we're working on the solutions.

***

So at the new mosque I had to effectively start again through revision. This began phase two of my journey.

It seemed like time had simply gone by - wasted. I was going through what I'd memorised again. I got to the 7th Juz fairly quickly. The initial teacher we had at this mosque left teaching us, but I'd finally got a teacher who I believed I would make progress with. He is without doubt amongst the most perfect Ḥuffāẓ I've met. Māshā'Allāh he is amazing. He didn't even need a second or backup Ḥāfiẓ during the Tarawīḥ prayers.

The reason I saw progress with him was that he did things others didn't: he spoke, suggested and advised. He saw potential and tried to nurture it as he took steps no one before had taken. He said to me I had to do three things:

1. I had to see him at the mosque before school [Fajr] sparing at least an hour for memorisation;
2. Lead the Tarawīḥ prayer in the final days of Ramaḍān; and
3. Always read the three things every day without fail - the new memorisation, the previous weeks or fortnights memorisation, and the revision of a Juz or a few Ajzā'.

I led my first Tarawīḥ prayer during that year reciting the 6th Juz. It was nerve racking and difficult. As I'd always been mistake-conscious with a perfectionist mentality - I didn't want to make mistakes in front of so many people. I did end up making some but it was a great experience. I am honoured and grateful for having had the chance to meet and benefit from that teacher. He was trying to show me how important it was to maintain memorisation.

Maybe he tried to get me used to reciting in prayers. It was funny, I even had to do a mock Tarawīḥ prayer. I had to recite and revise out loud pretending to lead the prayer. This is because reciting in prayer is different. There's the gap between each Qiyām and you can forget where you were reading.

Whilst this lasted, it was brilliant. We'd go in the mornings to read to him in a freezing cold office room. This wasn't consistent though. It was tough waking up for the guys. We often missed these sessions sleeping our way through the time.

It was unfortunate and inevitable that we were going to lose this teacher too. The teacher had to leave just like everyone else before him - everyone came and went. A game of "Musical Imams" started again. Just like the previous mosque, teachers came in and out. Just when I began to settle, it got ruined again!

No consistency with teachers meant that processes kept changing. New people have to get to know the students, but they might have other ideas - ideas that you weren't used to. Everyone brings their own dynamics to the equation.

At the last mosque we never really had a plan. We just went in and read our new part with some of the old. There was no concentration on the back portions. If you make sure in whatever you plan - even if it's a verse a day - to not miss a single day to recite something, you'll be on the right track.

They say that an apple a day keeps the doctor away, it's like that with the Qur'ān. You need to be consistent. So recitation every day keeps the memory in stay.

Don't neglect this.

TRIPLE DOWN ON YOUR STRENGTHS

"Success is achieved by developing our strengths,
not by eliminating our weaknesses."

— Marilyn Vos Savant

***

One of the things I was obsessed over was improvement.

As I've mentioned already, I have a thing about perfection. I think you need to be when it comes to the Qur'ān. Remember we're preserving the Words of Allāh. You need to be a perfectionist with its recitation too in order to avoid making errors. When I talk about strengths I mean all those things that help you memorise best and keep focused.

Weaknesses are important when it comes to personal or family life, but when you're taking on a project - it's your strengths that count. If you know what they are, knuckle down with them. Your teacher will help you recognise what they might be, (one of the perks of having a mentor) but you should be able to recognise them yourself too. Self recognition leads to the recognition of Allāh.

So what did I do?

I was at this mosque lasting a period of the final years of high school and two years of sixth form. So I had a lot of exams. I had a lot of homework. I was doing my GCSEs (US school diploma) and A-Levels (US APs). So naturally I was eager to finish before starting my university degree. I was getting busier.

So I began to experiment further with techniques. I had to find something to get me rolling quicker with only 2 hours a day to work with.

ANALYSING MY STRENGTHS

There was one thing I knew that I had - a strong connection to audio.

I remembered the days when I used to listen to Sūrah al-Rahmān and Wāqi'ah being played in the car; and how I used to recite the verses when we left the car. I remembered how I could recall verses after listening to 'Abdul Bāsiṭ. I thought about how I could imitate reciters and how I had the ability to playback in my head, as if I were hearing them in real time. I realised this was a major strength that I'd ignored all this time. I had to do something about it.

So I had a look on the internet for a device that I could use.

Back then, there wasn't any advanced smart technology we have the luxury of today. We had the good old Nokia's - the 6600's, or Motorola RAZR, or the Sony Ericsson phones. It was a different age. They were good times tough. Everything now is growing incredibly fast and increasingly everyone wants to do things faster. This is one of the elements that sets the stage for the coming of the Dajjāl as shayṭān loves to hasten. So I needed to find a device that would allow me to follow audio and text at the same time, and allow me to memorise better. I planned to use it as much as I could, particularly taking advantage of the time before and after classes.

I found something at last!

I constantly chased after my dad to get me a 'PenMan Digital Quran' (these were one of the first ones out). The problem was that they weren't available in the UK yet at the time. They weren't cheap either. So plan B was to buy or use tapes we had access to. I didn't like this option because it wasn't mobile enough. I had to play the tapes at home on the Hi-Fi. There was the option of using the Sony Walkman players, but I didn't have one. So I got by listening to verses here and there.

It took a while, but I finally got hold of a PenMan.

It may have cost around £100-199 GBP, it was difficult to convince my dad to get it for me but I had to push him. Once I'd got it I got experimenting right away. One of the drawbacks was that I wasn't allowed to take it into classes. I would have got told off, distracted others and laughed at. I know this because it happened with a teacher that I'm going to talk about soon. So what I did instead was to listen to the verses in bed before sleeping. I would repeat them and take them in after 10-12 repeats. I'd go on to the next verse and do the same. Then I'd combine them. This was all from the audio. I'd then go to sleep. It was a familiarity technique as well as an initial rough memorisation. I found it easier to memorise what I'd listened to. I know there are many people like this. You might be one of them.

***

How did I know that my memory was better served with auditory help? It was simple. I always remembered things that I heard. Not only the words but how they were recited. The speed, style and tune. Even now, I can replay portions in my mind and recite them exactly the same way as I first heard them.

There was an interesting incident in the first mosque.

At the time, I hadn't memorised Sūrah Taḥrīm, I wasn't anywhere near the 28th Juz. I recited the last verses of the Sūrah in a public gathering in the same way I had heard ʿAbdul Bāsiṭ ʿAbdus Samad recite them. The next day the teacher asked me about it out of the blue. He asked me to recite the same verses to him. This teacher didn't speak English, he spoke Urdu so I was going to have a hard time explaining what I had to say. I knew Urdu but didn't speak much of it fluently, likewise I knew Punjabi but never spoke much of it fluently.

I wanted to tell him 'I can only read it the way my brain plays it to me'. Really that is how it was. So what I had to do was press play in my mind, and then recite the words in the normal method I would recite to the teacher but I struggled. It was like trying to do two things at once. The teacher was surprised. He couldn't understand how I was able to recite the verses yet not know them. How could I have recited them without mistakes? He was as baffled as I was.

I didn't see this as a weakness, I saw it as a strength that needed nurturing but there was a problem. I had to learn how to transition those voices in my head into any mode of recitation. For instance, I know many people that can memorise fast and they read fast but, when they are asked to read slowly they can't do it. I figured out how I could get around things like this.

I started listening to different reciters with different speeds and styles - not for new verses but for verses that I already knew. I opened up my audio range if you like. This made it possible for me to be able to read in any style or speed. I changed the way I memorised and the melody I used. There are different strengths for everyone, you need to be able to recognise them for yourself. This is something I talk about in my upcoming book, *How We Memorised The Qur'ān: A Primer on Memorisation, Revision and Teaching.*

(Visit to sign up for the book: http://howtomemorisethequran. com/how-we-memorised-the-quran/)

So triple down on your strengths.

Keeping in mind that when you memorise verses, the way you do it stays with you. If you memorise them wrong, you've carved into the wall wrong. You then have a tough time fixing them. Make sure you memorise in the best and most perfect way in the first instance. This way, you will reduce mistakes and avoid having to constantly remove them. Try changing a habit of lifetime - it will take a long time but will require great patience.

AIM FOR MASTERY

*"Allāh loves a servant who when performing
a task does so skillfully."*

— Ḥadīth in Al-Bayhaqi

***

Following on from betting on your strengths, let's talk about something related. During a recent conversation with a teacher from the second mosque, he made a bold claim.

He said that if you memorise or revise the Qur'ān for four hours a day you will gain mastery in your memorisation. It made sense to me but others may need more time whilst others might not even have that kind of time. He simply said: "I guarantee you, anyone that wants to should take out 2 hours in the morning and

2 hours of the night. Inshā'Allāh they will have strengthened their Qur'ān."

So it got me thinking about achieving such mastery.

Mastery could be defined as Chambers defines it: "1 - usual mastery of something, a great skill or knowledge in it. 2 - especially mastery over someone or something, control over them or it."

Or we can define it in a different way by looking to the sacred language, Arabic. Let's look at a word mentioned in the Qur'ān once, mentioned by our beloved Messenger (peace and blessings of Allāh be upon him) and often by our scholars.

The Ḥadīth you just read at the start of this chapter uses a word from the Arabic word "Iṭqān". A word used for excellence or perfection. The word is used to show a level of quality. Some describe it as an "arrangement and disposition of things in a scientific and artistic way in order to get a perfect result." Interestingly the Arabic synonym for Iṭqān is Iḥkām which means to do something with wisdom. This creates a beautiful connection: reaching excellence through and with wisdom. This a clear sign of the concern that Islām has for producing quality work. And the Qur'ān is the Book of Wisdom, we reach excellence through it.

I've always understood Ḥifẓ to be a type of mastery. A mastery that has different levels to it. Not every Ḥāfiẓ is a master of its recitation for instance. Likewise, not every Ḥāfiẓ has complete mastery over its memorisation. For example, not everyone Ḥāfiẓ could recite to you just by giving them a page number, a paragraph number or a verse number. Everyone can't do that. So how does mastery apply to memorisation for us all?

Well simply put, aiming for the highest levels possible.

***

Here are some of the elements of mastery.

FINDING WHAT YOU'RE GOOD AT

I always advocate that people memorise by their strengths. Some of us are strong with visuals, some of us with audio, or combinations, or other means of learning. That is why I say to stop looking at your weaknesses. You waste an incredible amount of time trying to check those boxes. You are natural to and good at certain things for a reason. There are many ways to figure out what your strengths are but here is one method for doing this:

TAKE OUT A PAD

List everything you enjoyed doing from the ages of six to eighteen before your life was ruled by everything you do now. Or if you are between those ages have a look at what you enjoy. Since you were a kid you've loved at least something. Analyse what they have in common. Looking at myself for example I used to love the arts such as fine art and singing/reciting, and still do. Both involve creativity and intelligence. Reciting involves a strong case for listening skills - the first step to reciting is listening. Fine art involves patience, perfection and creativity. I combined both with my memorisation. I used my strengths of listening, reciting and did it in a creative way. Audit yourself, if you can't, ask somebody who knows you well and let them tell you who you are. Once you believe that for yourself, or once someone else has told you, go directly all-in into that. Bet on your strengths.

TIME: MEMORISE FOR FOUR HOURS A DAY

Back to what the teacher said. There's a reason those you hear about having mastery over something spend a good part of the day on that thing. Asking almost every master Ḥuffāẓ I encountered, how much time per day they spent mastering memorisation. They never gave an answer like: "I memorised twelve to twenty hours a day." Nothing as time-consuming as that. In fact, there are some people who completely dedicate time to the Qur'ān but they are rare gems, or those who went into it full-time. The typical answer I got was "I dedicated at least four hours of my time towards Qur'ān." They'd even do it when they'd already become Ḥāfiẓ revising over 4 Juz.

Typical recommendations are between 2.5 to 4 hours every day for 5 days a week.

Prominent behavioural psychologist Dan Ariely did research that tells us that the peak productivity period in a person's day is 2-5 hours after they wake up. After that, he says, there are declining returns to the work you put in. He says that "Generally people are most productive in the morning. The two hours after becoming fully awake are likely to be the best." His bottom line: "Your 'productive hours' are very important. Think about when those are, and then practice maniacal devotion to work during those hours."

STUDY THOSE WHO HAVE EXPERIENCE

In any area of life you want to succeed at, you have to study its history. All art is created in context. Studying the history of how previous world champions played and trained in any sport is critical toward figuring how you can improve on that training and play. In any business, studying the history of your focus industry, the biographies of the prior executives, and the successes and failures of those who went before you is critical for mastering that business. It's the same for memorisation of the Qur'ān.

This is one of the many reasons why it is so important to do your memorisation with an experienced Ḥāfiẓ. You get to probe them. You get to hear about things. But you'll be pleased to know we're trying to do this in a global Ḥifẓ community online - check it out! (http://howtomemorisethequran.com/hifdh/)

STUDYING YOUR FAILURES/BAD HABITS

Everyone always has something or someone to blame. They blame bad luck, black magic, evil eye, shayṭān, or whatever comes to mind. The key is to study each failure. You have to take notes about good times and bad times. You have to think about everything. Each failure or bad habit can teach you what to avoid when memorising.

GAINING EXPERIENCE

At some point, you have to do a certain amount of the same thing to get where you need to. In those thousands of repetitions of whatever, you will encounter many failures. A lot of people can play cricket a thousand times and never get better. Or bake a thousand cakes and never get better. You have to remember your experiences, study your failures, try to note what you did right and what you did wrong, and remember it all for future experiences. Future experiences will almost never be exactly like the old experiences. But they give you the ability to say, "Hmm, this is like the time four years ago when X, Y, and Z happened." And then you are engaging in . . .

USING PATTERN RECOGNITION

Being able to recognise when current circumstances are like an experience you've had in the past or an experience someone else you've studied had in the past is critical to mastery. Pattern recognition is a combination of all the above: study + history + experience + talent + a new thing . . . love.

LOVING IT

Andre Agassi has famously said he hated tennis. I believe this and I don't believe it. We all know that there are all kinds of love. There's unconditional love, which is hard to maintain. Then there's love that matures. There's a set of things you like about a person, even love. And sometimes you just fall out of love.

Do what your heart tells you to do. To become a master at anything there has to be love—so there will inevitably be much pain. And it can't be avoided. Nobody has avoided it. If something is too painful, then it's not the worst thing in the world to give up.

APPLYING POSITIVE PSYCHOLOGY

One reason most people in the world don't get really good at anything is because they don't want to put in the work. This is understandable. Often it's better to be social, have friends and strong family relationships and love people. But every master has the same psychy. They see beyond today.

How do you build that psychology? It can be a combination of a few things, including:

- Ego. The real belief that you can be the best, against all possible rational evidence to the contrary, against everyone trashing you simultaneously.
- Realising that there's a way out. If you ask many people what were they thinking when they were at rock bottom and the answer almost always was something like "I had to keep going!"

Which leads us to…

HAVING PERSISTENCE

Add up all the above and you get persistence. Persistence gets you experience. Persistence is a sentence of failures punctuated by the briefest of successes. Eventually, those successes will start to propel you toward mastery. Not one success or two. But many, many, many. How do you keep persisting when life is filled with changing careers, relationships, responsibilities, economic crashes, historical upswings, and so many things that can get in your way? There's no answer. That's why it's called persistence.

What matters is that you move forward and don't let the downturns get to you. Look after yourself health-wise: physically, emotionally, mentally, and spiritually.

Can you move forward today in each area?

Then you will attract mastery.

HALF WAY DONE

BUT IT'S TIME

TO LEAVE

EVERY TEACHER
HOLDS A KEY

*"I am a slave of him who teaches me one letter
of the alphabet."*

— 'Ali Ibn Abi Ṭālib
(May Allāh be well pleased with him)

***

Back to the story. Things were about to get a bit more serious.

I was getting to the end of high school. Exams were looming.
Sixth form college was next. I was taking a lot of time off mosque.
The worse part was that I wasn't feeling Ḥifẓ anymore. I began

to have doubts about whether I could do it. I began to feel a disconnection.

I remember I used to go out with my friends after school during year 11 (final year of the UK high school). I never used to do this before, but during that period I was getting pulled away from the mosque. We used to take ages walking back from school and then go to each others houses. Play around and goof around. At the back of my mind though was my memorisation. It was as if I was trying to find an escape route. I made it clear to my friends, I had to go to the mosque at some point. These were strange days for me. I was wasting time. I felt a little lost.

By the time I'd finished high school, I was approaching the 15 Juz mark. This was a testing period. Alḥamdulillāh speed wise things had improved markedly ever since I adopted the listening technique. Despite that, there was still an issue with revision. I was in danger of forgetting things once again. Teachers came in and out.

Finally though, we had some momentum with a teacher who seemed to be staying put. With him I stayed at the mosque till I'd completed 15 Juz (30th, 1st till 14th). His focus was on getting finished. He placed so much emphasis on it that under his supervision, I'd reached a level where I could memorise two pages a day within a three-hour timeframe. That was about 32 lines. I was using the 16-lined Tāj Company Urdu script Mus'ḥaf.

There was the same major problem though.

I hardly got time to revise.

I remember this year clearly. During the summer of my first year at college, I lived in the mosque. If it wasn't then it was the summer just before starting college. So I ate, slept, recited, laughed and played at the mosque. It was the teachers plan, I rolled with it. But things didn't go to plan. I don't know where things went wrong, but none of us got on with him so much.

The teacher had his tantrums and hardly spoke to me and another guy who joined me during the rest of the year. It was a distressing and difficult time. You can ask Mobin and Khurram about it :p

***

There was something that this teacher had changed in me.

As mentioned before, people tend to focus on time so much, he wasn't any different but his approaches were radically different.

He spoke to us but mocked us, he gave suggestions and tips but pranked us. Despite this, for the first time someone had pointed out things to us that we would have never noticed.

At times, he looked at things in a logical way, creating plans (forward-looking) and had a strict regime. He was all about structure and calculations. The biggest thing I learnt from him was that no matter how hard or stressful a teacher might be for you - each of them holds a key. They have experience.

By this stage, I probably had over 12 different teachers or more. I would've learnt something from each one. The single most important thing that will get you far will be respecting and honouring them. My dad always said to me, "Even if they taught you a single letter, respect them. They are your teachers and teachers are like fathers."

But this teacher, wow, he was something else.

I remember one time, we got up at Fajr and we had to read to him for an hour, but he was asleep. We stayed till the end of the hour in his room and left. Naturally we didn't want to disturb him but in the morning, he was furious with us. I said you were asleep so we didn't know what to do. At other times, he would force me to eat and drink things I didn't want to have - especially tea. I don't drink tea or coffee and he was the only guy who managed to get me to drink tea (and a certain type, they call it Dood Patti). I learnt a few cooking tricks though!

After the summer cut short, the rest of the year went pretty gloomy. I had stopped memorising. I wasn't allowed to move further until I had perfected the first half of the Qur'ān and rightly so. But there was no communication between the teacher and I. I never read to him either. He never bothered or at least didn't show it. I never took initiative though and that was my fault. He was probably expecting me to but I never did. But trust me, it was way too awkward.

That year was bad. It was stressful and depressing. I remember going to my parents and pouring it all out.

"I can't do this anymore. I've got my A-level stuff to do. But at mosque Shah Sāhib (the teacher) doesn't talk to me. Sometimes on rare occasion, he might talk but it's always a stab at me. There's nothing happening. I just go to the mosque and sit there for no reason. I try to revise till the end and leave. What's the point? And what's the point if I keep memorising and ignoring the past? I will keep forgetting it. Maybe the Qāri was right who said I should not do it. There is no point in carrying on."

I remember my mum telling me not to worry, things like this can happen. She recalled past doubts - what happened to those? She convinced me to carry on. Parents are also teachers. I remember my dad telling me something his guide once told him: "Go and serve your parents…they are your guides."

Try to find a mentor or teacher who you can sit with and find to be motivational and inspirational. There is nothing better than having someone there to hold you accountable but to also lend you a hand.

One thing is for certain, no matter what key a teacher holds if they are having a detrimental effect on your goals and motivations something has gone wrong. I knew this was the case for me. So for that entire year I was done. No more. I had to sort out the 15 Juz. So I began reading to my mum at home instead. During April in the year, I went on my first holiday to Cyprus and took some advice on going abroad for a year.

What happened was profound.

It made me who I am today.

Things were about to change.

EMBRACE THE MOMENTS
OF MOMENTUM

"The world is wide, and I will not waste my life in friction when it could be turned into momentum."

— Frances E. Willard

***

I had to make a decision.

I wanted to finish memorising the Qur'ān ideally before starting my law degree at university. I'd be having my final exams for my A-Levels in the summer. Luckily I had the option of taking a gap year before starting the degree. So after my trip to Cyprus in

April 2005, I decided to go to Egypt. My mind and heart was set in stone for Egypt. I had a passion for listening to reciters from the country. I already had an Azhari graduate hat given to me by my uncle. I had to go.

My parents gave me the go ahead.

I'd never been anywhere alone before. I was 17 and I didn't know anyone in Cairo either. I didn't know Arabic and I didn't have admission into a school there. Nothing was formal and I didn't even arrange a place to stay at either. I just wanted to go. I wanted to gain some mastery with the Qur'ān, even if I only had a year. So be it.

So I spoke to the head at the local mosque and he said I could meet an old Egyptian reciter who came annually to London. He is known as the Chief of Reciters, a legend and teacher of reciters - Shaykh al-Qāri' Aḥmad Muḥammad 'Āmir. So I went down for the 27th night of Ramaḍān that year to meet him. I recited that night at the mosque and then Shaykh Aḥmad recited after me. We met for the Saḥūr meal upstairs, an introduction was made and I was promised a meeting in Cairo to sort something out for me. So that was one contact sorted.

Then I got in contact with a professor at the American University of Cairo who was supposed to help me out - he gave me some advice over email. We talked about things to expect, contacts he had amongst other things. I was really impatient though due to the momentum I had. So much that I decided to book tickets without having any arrangements in place. I just knew something would happen. I loved the prospect of going somewhere without any arrangements too and doing it on the flow. There was something adventurous about that. I had the will, so surely there was a way.

A day or two before leaving, I found out that my friend's brother was studying in Cairo. In fact, I knew him so I called him the night before leaving. I asked him if he could pick me up at the Cairo airport. I remember him saying, "I don't remember who you are, but Inshā'Allāh I will get you from the airport, you can stay at my place until we find you a place to stay." I said something like "I know you, we've met before and I remember your face. Trust me, you'll know who I am when you see me."

A day later we meet at the Cairo airport. Funnily enough, he recognises me. I can't describe what I was feeling at the time. I'd flown on Czech Airlines. Had an awful pit stop at Prague. Got to Cairo safely with hardly any sleep. I can't sleep when travelling. We leave the airport and as I get into a taxi I feel a nice breeze. But it also begins to rain slightly but only where we stood. That's what I felt anyway - who knows - but I took it as a sign to tread carefully.

A journey was about to begin.

I'd secured my place at university for September in the following year so I had a year to learn Qur'ān, Arabic and whatever else I could learn.

I was buzzing. I had a chance to go to the land of the great 'Abdul Bāsiṭ.

I was there.

It was time.

***

Have you ever had a moment where you've felt so strongly about something that you were surging with ideas moving with excitement? Whatever you choose to call it - Eureka, the light bulb or lightening moment - these moments are usually things that spark momentum.

At certain times in your life, you just know that everything will change after it. You can ignore them and keep things the same. But if you take them head on your life path can alter permanently. It was at this unique moment in my life that was about to change everything. I could feel it.

When you're doing your Ḥifẓ you will go through ups and downs. No doubt about it. You've seen up till now how I'd gone through many ups and downs. It wasn't pitch perfect. It's important to capitalise on the good times. There will be days where you can memorise more easily than others. You'll have moments where you want to keep going. You'll have moments where you've achieved a milestone. All these create moments of momentum. You can embrace them by learning more or revising more. You can embrace them by sharing them with others.

I was at a point where I could have totally stopped.

I'd done half of the Qur'ān. Maybe it wouldn't have been so bad. That's a great achievement. But all big things start with small acts. So embrace the good moments, tread carefully in the bad ones. shayṭān is always wanting to draw us away from the task. It's funny, sometimes I hear people say you shouldn't leave the Qur'ān open because shayṭān reads it or shayṭān writes on the Qur'ān. Why would shayṭān want you to look away from it so that he can read it? He doesn't want to read, he's already got you looking away from it.

Remember that momentum keeps us going. All that said, at the same time you need to work reasonably with yourself. Do not overwork it or underwork it. Work with your capacity not against it.

This was my next lesson.

CREATE SEPARATION TO BUILD

"Focusing is about saying No."
— Steve Jobs

***

We got to the flat on the night of arrival.

It was a nice place and it had pretty much everything one would need. I wasn't entirely alone - I already knew two of the guys staying at the flat. I get shown around and prepare my bed for a good nights rest. I awake the next morning to see cockroaches on the floor.

Welcome to Egypt!

Next it was time for a nice breakfast. I get told to go out by the brothers to buy some bread. They gave me some money and for the first time, I'm about to see the daylight of Cairo. It was bright and it was hot. I needed some sunglasses! The shop was downstairs outside the building so I walk up to the shopkeeper and I don't know what to say. I missed that part. Even if I did I wouldn't have understood a word he'd say. So I ran back upstairs and asked 'how do I say I want bread again?' - 'Eyez Khubz!'. So I ran outside again and asked. Then I didn't understand what he was saying: "Gineh!" - so I went a back up and asked the boys what that meant - 'a pound!' [facepalm]. So I went back down and gave the man an Egyptian pound note. I thought it was funny when I heard this Arabic lingo, hearing things like "eyes" and what sounded like "guinea," I knew this was going to be an interesting journey.

I was now realising exactly what I was up against. I needed to learn the local language (called ʿĀmiyyah) and I needed to learn proper Arabic (Fushā).

I stayed at that flat for about two weeks learning whatever I could from the guys there. I'd use their laptops for researching and sending emails. We'd watch TV and try find my own accommodation. I'd also look to find a place or teacher to study with. Remember I hadn't made any plans for Cairo other than having a few contacts. So I had one of the boys tasked to arrange a meeting with the Qāri' Shaykh Aḥmad 'Āmir. It was around this point that I had flat arrangements made for myself.

I moved to a much poorer area in the eighth zone of Nasr City. At the time, there were two guys that were staying there. They too were Azhar University students. Amazingly I knew one of them too. Surprise surprise - he shared the same name as the brother who picked me up at the airport. I settled there and had my own bedroom. Conditions were not as good as the previous place. Electricity would go off, the water supply would go off, there were so many cockroaches in the morning and sometimes there was no water heating. Some things worked and others didn't. We had a TV we had to give a bang to work. The two brothers left to go back home pretty much straight away. So I was about to be completely alone.

I needed the help of one of the brothers before he left. I had to be taken around the area and find potential spots to begin studies. I visited the local mosque and a local Arabic school with him. He introduced me to teachers and got me in the know of how things worked. The local mosque, Masjid Rahman I think, had a 6-month Ḥifẓ programme. A class would run every 6 days. People would go in to read between 'Asr and Maghrib prayers.

I went down to read to the mosque Imām during one of those sessions. The brother from the flat explained my situation during the introduction and the Imām asked that I recite something. So I began from the Fātiḥa. He listened with attention. The boys around us were staring at me. I'm slightly nervous, but he says I recited well. He was surprised to hear someone recite like that especially from Britain.

He then asked me to continue reciting so I began Sūrah al-Baqarah. When I got to the fourth verse he interrupts saying, "Meyyyyy[n]" - I didn't know whether to laugh or pretend I knew what was going on. So I tried to repeat what he was saying. I had never heard of this before. So he said that although I had accurate pronunciation, because I hadn't studied Tajwīd certain rules were not being applied. He stressed, in particular, the different lengths, the Nūn Sākin rules especially the Ikhfā'. As I later found out that's what he was correcting me on - the Ikhfā'.

I was surprised at how no one ever told me about this before. I was even more surprised that I never picked this up whenever I listened to the Qur'ān. From that day, I began hearing all the intricate details all of a sudden. Whoever I listened to I looked carefully for the Ikhfā' and I picked it up in no time.

When I went to the local Arabic school 'Markaz Dād', the

teachers asked me to recite but this time I recited in Mujawwad - the way 'Abdul Bāsiṭ does in public. They were amazed and we spoke about arranging Arabic classes. I eventually started doing Arabic with Ustādh Rabī', one of the teachers there, one-on-one for around two hours a day early at Fajr. I should have been learning Qur'ān at Fajr instead but I looked at it from another angle. If I went to do Arabic at Fajr when it was quiet, I could get more done whilst being at my sharpest so I could learn more. Not only that, I could apply what I learnt throughout the whole day. We would do conversation, listening, writing and reading in each session. Just within a month, I'd finished the Arabic text and was able to hold conversations with people. Although I could converse it wasn't without a struggle. I often understood more when people spoke to me but couldn't respond with many words in Arabic. I just had to build my vocabulary.

I had an exam after I finished that text. The exam involved dictation, writing, reading and listening. It went well. I got around 47 out of 50 marks, something like that. It was time to go up another level. He wanted me to start another text so I did.

It then occurred to me, I needed to create separation in order to build on my Ḥifẓ.

I decided to stop taking the Arabic classes not too long after we started the second text. We probably did near half of it. It was about a month and a half that I'd studied Arabic with him. Besides certain issues that prepped up with the teachers, I thought I'd done enough to get by as far as language was concerned. I knew how to use the dictionary so I could build on vocab. I watched some Arabic TV to improve on things too. I remember meeting Ustādh Rabī' in the streets one day and he was surprised I'd learnt more Arabic. I said I watched TV!

Reflecting back on the decision, I made a huge mistake. I should have made alternative arrangements to make my schedule easier and more focused. At the time though I was thinking emotionally and financially. I thought the Arabic would have gotten harder as we started going more into grammar. It meant more work in a small time frame. The Ḥifẓ arrangements were made which meant I had to travel a lot. Could I deal with memorising for many hours, travel, cooking, Arabic classes, homework and exams? I wasn't too sure.

So I decided I had to take it easy. Focus on what mattered to me at the time.

There's something important to mention here - learning Arabic will help you memorise better. There are certain verses that follow a certain pattern but change certain words, when memorising those people can get mixed up or forget things. When you understand the language though, it makes sense and you know what's what and where's what. The period I learnt Arabic certainly helped me. Try it, you'll notice a difference. When I got back in 2007, I began to study Arabic further.

***

When I was memorising during high school and college I could have been distracted by friends.

I could have gone to join after school clubs and go out to events. — I said no.
I could have joined school sports teams. — I said no.
I could have said no to the mosque. — But I said yes.

I needed focus.

I already had to focus on school work, but I had to attend the mosque too. I knew my progress wasn't amazing. If I took on extra things after school it would have added to the pressure of finishing memorisation. If I joined other things with friends my attention towards the Qur'ān would have grown weaker.

Some of the students memorising with me have joined after

school clubs. I always tell them, I never did it. If you truly want it, you have to create separation. You need separation to build until it's built.

For most of us, we're busy with studies or with work. Outside that world we're busy with family lives, but how do you achieve something you want to do like Ḥifẓ? You need to create some sort of separation. Everyone differs according to their situation, but there is always a way to do something you really want. I really wanted to get my Ḥifẓ done so I created separation from the 'busyness' of the UK life to the different world of Egypt. They say that tourists see and travellers seek. I was both a see'er and a seeker.

What can you do to create separation to build on a dream?

It could be taking out an hour split into two half hours within the day where you keep yourself to yourself to memorise and revise. Try something at the very least. It's just about making a portion of the day sacred for memorisation. In that portion you wouldn't do anything else; everything will be zoned out.

When I said I had to take it easy. That's important. Why? If you create separation and try to make every second count toward building the goal you can get worn out.

You can also get so immersed into it that you ignore everything else that is important. Your health or your family for instance. I know this all too well. I often get involved in so many things because I know time is limited. Think about lifting weights, you work your muscles and create small tears in ways that help grow them in size and strength. You need recovery which is as important as the work you put in. Realising this, I had to make a good plan. A plan that allowed me to use the time to rest, rejuvenate, and reconnect with things I cherished most.

It's important to allow yourself to be a human being, rather than a human doing.

TIME FOR
A FRESH
START

TAKE STEPS
WITH PURPOSE

"You have to have a big vision and take very small steps to get there. You have to be humble as you execute but visionary and gigantic in terms of your aspiration."

— Jason Calacanis

***

I was now in a situation having around 10-11 months to complete memorisation of the Qur'ān.

I had to walk with purpose everywhere I went and with anything I did. I decided to make a plan for the first time. I never had a

Ḥifẓ plan before, no targets or anything. The last teacher I had a tough time with opened me up to this idea. He actually made me a plan himself to memorise two pages a day to finish the second half of the Qur'ān within a few months.

So when I was in Cairo I mapped out a plan to memorise 3 pages a day 6 days a week. I'd use the 7th day for revision and to re-energise. My Qur'ān had 18 pages per Juz so I worked out if I had done 3 pages a day, I'd complete a Juz every 6 days. That's about 4 Juz every 24 days.

I wanted to ideally complete Ḥifẓ in 6 months and use the other 6 months to do it all again. The idea behind that was to combine solidification with revision. I'd already memorised half in the UK, but I had to start again. I wanted to start afresh; that is why I like to say I memorised within a 6-month period. So memorising the 30th, the 1st Juz till the 14th should be really easy. For the rest I would have to see how it goes. I knew some of it was going to feel like I was doing it from scratch, even though I had memorised them before.

With the plan sorted I needed someone to do it with.

So I started at the local mosque. I'd go in and read a 1/4 of a Juz every day for the first couple of Juz as I knew them pretty well. I thought if I boxed off 6 Ajzā' I could easily do the rest within 6 months doing 3 pages a day. It was going to be a huge challenge. But I thought if I memorised a page in an hour before school, a page in the evening when I was in the UK, surely I should be able to do 3+ a day over in Cairo? It would all be down to me.

During this period, we finally arranged a meeting with Shaykh Ahmad 'Āmir at his house. I remember going down to a house near the headquarters of Al-Azhar. We went in and it was a classic looking place. We got chatting and he asked me to recite something. I recited a few verses from the second Juz. Unfortunately, he couldn't teach me himself but he wanted to make some introductions. So we arranged to meet at one of his weekly public Qur'ān circles in the grand mosque of Imām al-Hussain (peace be upon him). These circles take place in every grand mosque of Cairo with leading Qur'ān reciters appointed to attend each one by the government. It was an honour for me to go down so I invited friends to go with me.

When we got there people were taking turns to recite from the Mus'haf. The teachers would make corrections. In the end, Shaykh Ahmad asked me to recite again. He said, "Recite what you recited at my house. The same way." He began introducing me to the other reciters and teachers. He's a great guy and was full of praises. I was nervous. I was next to the chair where the top reciters sit to recite at events and weekly at the Friday prayers. In the mosque of Imām al-Ḥussain, I was nervous and so I closed my eyes and started. As soon as I finished I began to get a load of pats on my back and people greeting me. It wasn't recorded, but I don't think I've read those verses the same ever again. It's like when you cook something really well and you can't do it the same again.

We then went into the head office and common room of the mosque, everyone was being served tea. It's a nice common room. Everyone was sat around the room. You can learn more about the mosque of Imām Ḥussain in this video (https://www.youtube.com/watch?v=MzIK-4fVdaw) where you can see the office space. I was then introduced to the Qāri' who Shaykh Aḥmad had talked about at his house. It was someone called Shaykh al-Qāri 'Abdul Rāziq Ṭahā 'Ali. He was from the Khikhiya Mosque situated in the heart of Cairo - Opera Square - one of the most historic mosques in the old city built by the Ottomans. Though at the time he was posted to be at Masjid Imām al-Ḥussain on the most part during the weekdays (between Sunday and Thursday). He used to make the Aẓān, recite the Qur'ān, and lead the prayers at the mosque. He had an incredible character and impeccable behaviour. His voice was strong and his memorisation of excellent calibre. There's a video on YouTube (https://www.youtube.com/watch?v=n_2EkasM

Bvc&feature=youtu.be&t=2m56s) from the mosque, you can actually hear his Aẓān in it.

***

There was another brother with us who wanted to read with Shaykh ʿAbdul Rāziq too. He's a teacher and Imām now in the UK. I didn't make a decision right away whether I should read to him or not. He didn't ask for money or anything, all I had to do was be prepared to travel up to 30 minutes every day to get to him. They said I could come on a Wednesday. I was happy to proceed, but I was thinking more local at the time. I ended up going both to him and locally.

So I arranged to meet him in his room at Masjid Imām al-Ḥussain on a Wednesday. It was tiring. In the UK, it was the equal of travelling to another city. I was travelling across the busy areas of Cairo to read some pages of the Qur'ān. It had to be done. He would call me 'Shaykh Muḥammad' and would always greet me as one of his own. He was special. I'd never had this type of relationship with a teacher before. They honoured their students and sat with them in a down to earth manner. Gave them space, offered them food and invited them. All which never happened in the UK.

So what kept me going? It was taking each step with purpose.

Each time I travelled I revised or recited. I made a daily routine around my purpose: memorisation. I didn't manage time, I managed focus. I didn't do anything that didn't help contribute towards the goals of the day. I never went out to eat except on my self-imposed day off - Fridays. Otherwise, I would cook a dish at home. When I'd cook I tried to recite too. When I'd go out I'd try to recite. And I remember carrying a pocket Mus'haf which I'd never done previously due to the respect of the Qur'ān. Even when I was in the UK, I'd be reciting at school and someone would ask: what are you singing?

Don't forget your purpose.

My purpose was to:

(1) complete the memorisation of the Qur'ān and so in fulfilling my parents dream gaining the pleasure of Allāh;
(2) prove myself;
(3) prove my ex-teacher wrong who said I would never memorise the Qur'ān when I left for Cairo. I had a phone call from my dad whilst out there and he'd told me this was what he said. I reminded my dad it's hearsay as he never heard it from him personally, but he is entitled to say as he wants.

Time will tell.

SURROUND YOURSELF WITH PEOPLE THAT MAKE YOU BETTER

"If you want to go fast, go alone. If you want to go far, go together."

— African proverb

***

Praise be to Allāh, I never met anyone detrimental or of a bad influence on me in Cairo amongst the locals.

Eventually I was joined by an intelligent brother from the UK who was already a Ḥāfiẓ. He stayed with me in the flat. He would always ask about how I was doing (with Ḥifẓ), and if I needed help he was available. He came to study Arabic and further his studies from there. Māshā'Allāh he is now a teacher and Imām. I made friends with local Egyptians who would always speak in English but force me to speak Arabic. Even though, I'd get away with speaking English most of the time. They'd always ask about how things were going with the Qur'ān memorisation. So it was good.

Living in Cairo with no family around I could have done anything I wanted. I could have gone elsewhere instead of reading the Qur'ān and when the brothers asked how things were going I could have been the best liar in the world.

Yes. There were plenty of distractions and temptations there. I wasn't used to having sunny days all the time. My home town, Manchester is spectacularly random with the weather with most days pouring rain. Whenever it's sunny you want to go out, and whenever it's gloomy you don't want to go anywhere. So it was difficult in that sense to keep focused. Especially when you like an adventure.

My mission though was clear and I needed to keep at it.

There was one guy who helped me more than anyone else whilst I was out there. He was an important figure not only for me but for many brothers. Everyone knew him in the student circles. If it wasn't for the new roommate though I may never have met him. Networks are important after all.

This guy had been in Cairo for several years, (in fact he is still there at the time of writing) having done a degree, a Masters, a PhD and more. He was well versed about everything. He is also a great Ḥāfiẓ. I have to call him doctor and a father now, Māshā'Allāh. I first met him the day the new flatmate arrived. He's the type of guy who smiles all the time and loves a laugh. When I was ill despite living a long distance away from him, he was there. He was there to advise and take me around. He showed me the ins and outs. When I needed a place to stay when I returned to Cairo the next summer (yes I went back again) he offered me one of his places to stay in until I got a place sorted. He gave me books and a lot more. He used to love conversations that involved much reflection. So one thing that he always did was talk about the past. I appreciated that and I knew others said he did it too much, but someone with such experience was going to be of benefit to me. I listened. I got to teach him some English too.

***

So whilst in Cairo, I had to make sure I was surrounded by people that would help me further my ambitions.

Certain people help you see things that you could never have envisioned without their influence. Having the presence of people that are smarter, kinder, wiser, and different from you that enables you to evolve. People that make you think years ahead. Those are the people to surround yourself with at all times.

When you are memorising the Qur'ān or whatever you are doing, you need to surround yourself with these types of people. People that won't take you further from your goal but keep you on your toes.

Company. It's crucial.

Today we have company everywhere through the connectivity of the internet and the internet of things. There's an increasing number of 'influencers' through various mediums. PC, desktop, laptop, smartphone, tablet, apps, video, audio, books, games, movies - you name it. All these things are 'company'.

As you read this book you are in my company.

When you read a book or any work you are in the company of the author. Which is why we should read the Qur'ān more and more to be in the Great Company, Allāh, Most Generous. So I'll say it again, surround yourself with people that make you better.

DON'T RUSH THINGS, TAKE CALCULATED STEPS

"Consideration is from God, and haste is from the devil."

— The Messenger of Allāh
(peace and blessings of Allāh be upon him).

***

When I reflected on my time at the two mosques in the UK I noticed something.

Each time that I rushed something, I had to work that much harder to keep it. Every time I increased the amount I memorised

I had to train my brain to adjust. No matter what, every time I had to work two or three times harder to keep it. How do you train your brain to do that?

All I can say is that you do it so much that it becomes programmed into it.

The first time I had to start memorising two pages a day I found it easy memorising. It looked something like this:

1. Read before sleeping to get familiar with the new portion with the audio. I wouldn't fall asleep until I'd done the whole page.
2. Wake up at Fajr or in the morning hours before school and go to read to the teacher at the mosque.
3. When memorising I would do a verse at a time or a line at a time. I'd repeat it until I could read it fast without looking. For me, this was a sign that my brain had familiarity and the memory was being to stick. As for repetition I initially used to do 11, then I read somewhere that the brain was good with 21-22 so I did that. Recently I came across a method that mentions it's best to stick to odd numbers,

preferably 99 or 33. Eventually, I didn't care about the numbers. I cared about knowing it even if it took 100 times repetition. This is important actually, there's no set formula. Just keep repeating until you know it firmly.

4. I'd then move on to the next verse or line, do the same and combine it with the previous. I'd do this till the end of the page. It would take around 30-45 mins to memorise 16 lines.

5. I'd then read it to the teacher and leave for home, go school.

6. Come back from school and go to the mosque.

7. Revise over what I recited in the morning first and start memorising the next page. In the evenings, this was always harder. It was a real mission at times. In fact, I didn't get time to listen to the audio for the second page. If I did, it was only familiarity. At times too I would forget what I'd learnt in the morning so I'd have to adjust.

8. I finished a Juz in 9 days for the first time. It was Juz 14.

This was the first time I'd done something with such speed. And guess what?

I didn't know the Juz too well.

My brain simply wasn't used to it yet. It was overdone. It was too quick and too much to take in. Because I'd focused on trying to do 2 pages a day most of my time went into that. The revision was then compromised. My teacher made a plan for me to finish Ḥifẓ that year. This was when everything came crashing down. My confidence went downhill and I began doubting myself.

The solution was there, if I had thought about it I would have seen it. I had to increase my repetition or quadruple it. I had to do this by taking more breaks and recall the verses more often. I would have had to add another hour for revision.

The plan in Cairo was to learn three pages forget about two. So I had to think over this carefully. I couldn't and shouldn't be repeating the same mistakes again.

Taking the weight lifting analogy. You can't take on a lot of weights when you're not ready. Progression is calculated progression. You have to work yourself hard but not too hard. Just enough not to damage yourself. In the same way, when you take on a lot with memorisation, you're putting weight on top of weight. Your brain will be forced to drop some of it along the way. You think you've memorised it but you haven't. So take a calculated approach.

***

So what was my master plan?

Execution. Execution. Execution.

I had my father coming to visit for two weeks with friends for a Ḥifẓ completion ceremony scheduled in June 2006. I had to complete it by then. If I had a mechanism in place to be accountable for it, this was it.

I would read from ẓuhr till Maghrib. The times were something between 12pm till 6pm. Six hours with a break. I could memorise the three pages within the time frame on most days, it wasn't easy. I did so much repetition it was unbelievable.

For inspiration, I'd meet many people in al-Azhar and around Cairo memorising. I'd meet young memorisers and old. I'd get asked for advice and I'd ask for advice. I would get exposed to different techniques. I experimented until I was comfortable. The only thing I couldn't do was rush the memorisation.

If I completed it in 6 months, I knew I had a further 6 months to repeat it so I would hopefully be in a good position. 6 months is a short time and it is more or less rush time. Instead I thought I could memorise whatever amount I could whilst out there to perfection and carry on when I returned to the UK. But this option wasn't going to click with my dad. I wasn't going to mention it.

When you're memorising just remember - don't rush things just for the sake of a date. Instead get things right for the sake of doing it right.

ACCEPT AND LEARN FROM YOUR MISTAKES

"Success does not consist in never making mistakes but in never making the same one a second time."

— George Bernard Shaw

***

Progress wise, things had started well and memorisation was going well. I'd learnt Arabic, enough to speak, converse, write, read and understand most things. I could also understand much of the Qur'ān.

At this point in the story, I was up to the 13th Juz reciting and memorising Sūrah Ra'd. I couldn't help but think about how I was feeling: annoyed. I was memorising something that I'd already done over a year ago, but it felt like something new. It was like day one again. I always tell my students today "make mistakes, it's the best thing you can do as long as you accept and learn from them. Without mistakes, you're not human and you won't grow. Don't see it as a bad thing." But that's the main issue, learning from them and not doing it again. Sometimes we become habitual to certain things and we keep making the same mistakes.

At this moment, I was accepting that I made mistakes of not having a rigorous revision system in place. Even if I did have one I never stuck to it. It's the way everything seemed to be going. It was why I felt I should quit. This was another important junction of the journey. I could continue to memorise without solidifying anything and so repeat the greatest mistake any memoriser could make. Or I could re-organise my day, fess up to my mistakes and do this the proper way. It needed focus, it needed a system and it needed passionate determination.

My typical day at the time would have looked like:

- Get up for Fajr (sometimes falling asleep straight after and sometimes staying up)

- If I stayed awake I'd go for a walk or run outside, have breakfast and start reading.
- If I went to sleep, I'd wake up again sometime before ẓuhr. Have breakfast or brunch.
- I'd start memorising after lunch all the way till 'Asr prayer.
- Rush out to go on the 30 min drive to Al Azhar mosque and Masjid Imām Ḥussain to recite to Shaykh 'Abdul Rāziq. If the Shaykh wasn't there I'd revise inside the mosque (amazing experience) or go back home.
- 30 mins later I'd be catching up with the flatmate talking about our days.
- Cook dinner, or eat leftovers.
- If there was something on TV, we'd watch it.
- I'd get tired and go to bed.

I needed to change something immediately.

Even my flatmate reminded me - don't forget the revision! This is something that so many Ḥuffāẓ struggle with today. Many get by fine revising once a year for the Tarawīḥ prayer, but others struggle and forget quicker. They don't stick to any revision plan. They start and stop. What they have to identify are the issues preventing them from not sitting down to revise.

If you looked at the day above I bet you could tell me what I should have done differently. Do the same with your own days. I ask my students to keep a daily, monthly and yearly account of their progress. We've modelled it after the Bullet Journal (productivity) and the Five Minute Journal (positive psychology). It's a model of Muḥāsabah - retrospection, which is something we've lost in our times. As attributed to the great 'Umar ibn al-Khaṭṭāb: "Bring yourself to account before you are taken to account."

You can read further about the journals here: http://howtomemorisethequran.com/hifdh-management/

LOOKING AT THE DAY:

I can't avoid the commutes but I'm wasting time at Fajr. Maybe sleeping too much. There's not much physical activity, wasting time watching TV and so not using my time after dinner well. I could easily use Fajr for memorising, take a break, do physical activity, eat and re-energise. Start memorising at ẓuhr till 'Asr with a break or two. Go on the commute and read at the same time (easier if not in a taxi). Dedicate the night to revision. Perhaps this is what I should have done, and I did. I even started going to a gym in Cairo courtesy of guest perks!

I was still having problems though, sometimes I would miss the evening revision - too tired, or we went out or something. Sometimes I'd miss Fajr reading because of a long previous day. There was no consistency. This even happens at home too. So what are you supposed to do?

After filtering the good and bad, you could put yourself to account with stakes on it. "If I don't do such and such a thing [name] will do such and such a thing" - you make an agreement and you are put to account for it. You can try to find ways to get it right, but that will be risky. You can keep going in circles. In my case, I wish I had done the former but I didn't do the latter either, I changed the system of the day.

If you manage focus rather than time, time will manage itself. In a world full of temptations and distractions, prioritisation of focus is immensely important. You create separation to build remember? So that's what I did. Instead of looking at what wasn't working, I optimised what was working and looked at when I was memorising/revising to my best levels. If I could figure this out, I could build on that and do better.

I already knew before sleeping I was good with audio so I had to bring that back into the system. I knew that I was fresh when I woke up at Fajr, but my body needs good sleep so I'd keep that for reciting certain Sūrah instead. I knew that between midday and sunset I wasn't at my peak so I divided it between the new and the old. This way anything that remained I could do it before sleeping. This worked much better.

***

CONSISTENCY IS EVERYTHING.

The Beloved Prophet (peace and blessings of Allāh be upon him) is reported to have said, "The most beloved of deeds to Allāh are those that are most consistent, even if it is small".

When you're memorising sometimes you might say things like: 'it's ok - I can do it tomorrow,' or 'I already know it' or 'I can't'. These are often just words. What it translates to is missing a day without any reading whatsoever. Missing a day without revision. Missing a new memorisation for the day. Not wanting to do something. All of these sort of things tie into mistakes you'll make.

Before moving on, make sure you never miss a single day, whether it be something new (even if it is a little) or revision. The mistakes I made were over consistency. It was my perseverance and determination that got me through it and even today the journey still continues. Mistakes force you to pause, evaluate, and iterate. Mistakes are important. It often accelerates achievement. Make sure you pause, test, and iterate.

In certain situations, you wish there could be a sign to guide you to the right direction. Sometimes you call to Allāh, "Show me O Lord!" and He shows you. But sometimes you have to look within. Amazingly the signs are always there. We don't often seek them or even see them. Our eyes are closed. Once we open them, we can see them.

When you're memorising you will wish for signposts. You will get signs, but you need to read them along the way. Signs that will tell you to change your approach and to revise certain portions. Signs to ask a question, signs to recite more, signs to change environment or company. All these you will have to listen to. It's part of the calculated steps.

Note shayṭān is smart. If he can't get you to move away from the Qur'ān, he can use the Qur'ān against you to get you to move away from the Qur'ān. You think you're memorising a lot, you're doing well, you're thinking about the end goal: I'm going to finish in 6 months. All the while though shayṭān is making you concentrate on just on the figure goal. And then constantly making you change it so that you eventually don't do it at all. Or worse still, he wants you to do it because he knows you'll find it hard to keep. This is why we always say "I seek refuge with Allāh from the cursed Satan" every time we begin to recite. Never forget it.

But we don't blame things on shayṭān. We take responsibility because that's what makes us different. That is what allows us to get better and open the doors to the mercy of Allāh.

YOU ARE HERE TO
BUILD AND TEACH

"You are here in order to enable the world to live more amply, with greater vision, with a finer spirit of hope and achievement. You are here to enrich the world, and you impoverish yourself if you forget the errand."

— Woodrow Wilson

***

I referred to a 'game' of 'Musical Imāms' being played at the mosques I used to go to. You remember?

Musical Imāms meant that sometimes we never had a teacher in attendance at one of the classes. Somehow I ended up taking over those classes even though I was supposed to be a student trying to memorise. How many times did my journey have to be disrupted? Seriously.

I don't remember this happening at the first mosque but it did happen at the second. It was a interesting experience. Effectively, I was being self-taught to teach. This was my first exposure to teaching. I was in high school.

The first class I had to take over was the young children's class. I think those aged between 5-9. It was fun, but it was tough. Understandably, I didn't want to teach because of my Ḥifẓ. But it did give me an excuse to get away from it. It was an experience I learnt a lot from. I got an opportunity to reflect on how things were done at the mosque, what things were done wrongly and how things could be improved. I learnt the most when I had to monitor the Qur'ān reading class. I saw how beneficial teaching was in my own development. It forced me to know my stuff but also learn even more.

Students can ask you questions about something you'd never thought of. When you're speaking to them you might be inspired to speak about the topic from an angle that you'd never thought of before. For those memorising, you get a chance to make your memorisation stronger through teaching others.

I began teaching from home whilst I was still memorising at the second mosque. We'd get the young boys and girls of the family together in a informal setting. We'd get each one to do something: recite Qur'ān or poetry, talk about something and answer questions. We'd talk about things they wanted to talk about and we'd eat what they wanted to eat. Soon after that I started teaching Qur'ān reading, basic Islamic knowledge, alongside discussions on current topics. When I came back from Cairo in 2006 I had my first set of students who'd finished Qur'ān and had learnt several other things with me. I've been teaching ever since part-time for free almost every day. Small, personal and fun sessions first held at my house, or cousins house, then moved to a local hall and then to a friends house using his community space where I currently teach.

**

Whilst in Egypt I took every opportunity to teach something to somebody.

I taught English here and there, I took people on tours and I advised Qur'ān students. I was invited to a student organised gathering in the Azhar university students hostel. It was full of scholars, scholars-to-be, teachers, teachers-to-be, students and common folk like me. It was beautiful with people of all backgrounds in attendance.

I was invited to recite some Qur'ān to start the gathering. I recited Sūrah al-Duhā that day. I recited it in a combined style of 'Abdul Bāsiṭ and Muṣṭāfā Ismā'īl. The people received me well. Afterwards, a group of students came around me for a chat. They were a great lively bunch. They started asking me questions about my origins, what I was doing and where I lived. One of the brothers really insisted that I taught them about recitation and Ḥifẓ. They spoke about their problems. I took the opportunity to give some quick advice, but I had to leave with his number on my phone.

At another point I travelled to go and read to Shaykh 'Abdul Rāziq, but he wasn't there so I stuck around revising. When I chose to leave I came across a guy outside the door peeking into the mosque. He was a tourist so I spoke to him. It went something like this.

"Hey, how's it going?" I said.
"Yeah, not too bad thanks[…]" in a familiar accent.
I see him with a bike, so I ask "Is this your bike?"
"Yeah, I've actually come from Canada on it," he says.
"What?! Really?" I say completely astonished.

"Yup, I'm going out of here on the bike too across Egypt."

Impressed by what I hear, naturally I wanted to know more. So I start to tell him a little about what I was doing there and we got to know each other a little. He was an epic traveller so I asked him whether I could show him around. He welcomed the prospect of going into the mosques and seeing Islamic heritage.

He said, "They won't let me in the mosque though because I'm not a Muslim."

So I said, "That's not right, I'll take you with me."

So I went to take him inside the mosque of Imām al-Ḥussain first, as we were just outside the mosque. As soon as I was about to take him in an Egyptian inside approaches and says stop. It is prohibited to bring in that man - he is not a Muslim. I basically ignored him whilst telling him that he was categorically wrong. I was going to take him inside as long as he took his shoes off. I was going to do it and they couldn't stop me. I thought how have we gone this low. Not allowing the community to enter the Masjid and worse not allowing our sisters to enter.

So I took him in and gave him a tour. We sat down and talked further about things. I then took him inside the Maqām area of the mosque where it is believed that the blessed head of Imām al-Ḥussain is (or had been). Here I was confronted again by a bunch of Egyptians. This time I had to back off a bit, it was inside the mosque and I knew better. So I took him out and left the mosque. We then went to the Al-Azhar mosque to have a look around that.

Before he left I asked about the bike again and how on earth he was going to ride through Cairo. The traffic is insane over there. He had bags of confidence though. "I've gotten this far so I suppose I'll manage". Amongst his final words were that he'd learnt a lot through meeting me and was very grateful. All I wanted to do was take the opportunity to learn something and give something. Through giving, we receive so many blessings. I hope that one day he'll remember what a young Muslim who he never knew was like to him. Though one might think he'll likely remember what the Egyptians did to him more.

***

So what has this to do with our journey?

The truth is that it has everything to do with it.

Apart from fulfilling our purpose to Allāh, we are here to build and teach. Through memorising the Qur'ān, you sort of become a guardian of the Words of Allāh. The Prophet (peace and blessings of Allāh be upon him) said, "Indeed the best of you is the one who learns the Qur'ān and teaches it." I always like to say this can potentially apply to anyone. Say you've memorised certain verses, chapters or passages from the Qur'ān. You've then learnt what they mean. You then try to understand them. You then begin to make mention of them in conversations. You've done just as the Ḥadīth says. Imagine then if you learnt the entire Qur'ān and taught it. This was the way the noble companions used to memorise the Qur'ān. They would memorise first, then begin to repeat it in order to understand it to a point that they could now implement it. Once they implemented it, they moved on to memorising the next verses.

Why can't this apply when you are memorising?

It will strengthen your memorisation through connections. Teaching something creates a stick'ivity effect. The topic being taught becomes something you retain better and teaching it repeatedly teaches you in return. Take the opportunity then to help others memorise, memorise in pairs, and memorise in groups.

This principle doesn't only apply to the Qur'ān, it applies to everything.

The opening quote summed it up nicely. "You are here in order to enable the world to live more amply, with greater vision, with a finer spirit of hope and achievement."

Think about those coming after you. What could you do today that will create the stepping stones of something you built or taught.

TRICKY TIMES

DON'T MULL OVER
THE BAD TIMES

"No one really has a bad life. Not even a bad day.
Just bad moments."

— Regina Brett

***

I had so many days where I struggled to memorise.

I couldn't memorise as much as I could on those days. You might have had the same experience before. Even situations where you've memorised (so you think) and you take a break, you return to it to only find that you've forgotten it. Those types of days can get to some of us and trust me, you will have them.

We'll try so hard to memorise, keep reading and reading trying to get it all in. These situations are usually not about a connection to the Qur'ān. What do you think? They're about cramming in whatever you have to because of your plan or because you were told to. They're about trying to memorise whatever the situation might be. For me, these were signals. You have to recognise them as they come along in your own journey.

What do I mean by 'signals' anyway?

Our brains can only take on so much. We have natural body indicators that tell us to stop and rewire. These are the signals. It's the source that's the issue here - not your memorisation.

Thinking over the bad times is not fruitful for your state of mind and well-being. It will stress you out. Interestingly whilst some research has shown that it can make the brain smaller, stressing out about stress is the actual problem. All you do is regret things instead of thinking about how to rewire the situation. I'm going to tell you two or three things that could work for you on the difficult days.

MEDITATE (OR MURĀQABAH)

Take time out. Your brain will likely be drained, and needs recharging. Meditation super-charges your brain because it's essentially a practice in focusing your attention. Focus takes practice; you can't just make it happen when you need it if your mind doesn't know how to do it. It allows the parts of your brain that process massive amounts of information (your frontal lobe, parietal lobe, and thalamus) to take a break. Less anxiety. Mindful meditation (literally sitting and doing nothing) is shown to increase the brain's ability to filter out distractions. This means your brain is able to synthesise new information and recall old information more effectively. So it's good for the memory.

TAKE A NAP

The Prophet (peace and blessings of Allāh be upon him) had the habit of taking a siesta. It's doable for those who have the time or ability to do it but, whenever you face this situation you should take a nap if you're able to. According to research, it not only improves memory but solidifies it. If you can't memorise, stop reading and return to it at a later point.

TAKE A BREAK AND PLAY

Exercise is amazing for our bodies, but it's also good for our brains. When you exercise, it activates a "stress mode" in your brain and tells it to produce a protein that has a reparative element for your memory neurons. As for a "flight or fight" scenario, exercise is optimising your ability to do either by "resetting" your memory to only remember what is most important. Exercise also increases your sensory input and prepares your brain (and body) to deal with the stress it is experiencing. That's why exercise is linked to mental alertness.

***

Truth be told. Most of us think we can't do any of these things, but you can. Let's take the example of students at a class.

If you're memorising and you can't do anything. You feel like your brain is overloaded. You can start meditating sat where you are. Close your eyes, go quite and relax. Just hear the sounds around you and think of nothing. There's another thing though, what about if the source is being tired - what then? In this case, I have done two things: either stop reading or do something creative to get around it. The Prophet (peace and blessings be upon him) advised us to stop reading the Qur'ān is you are tired too because in that situation you find that your "heart is not attached" to it.

Brain research has also suggested that when you are at an optimal level you are wired to work and produce your best work. But when you are tired you are more creative. The brain when tired can't filter out distractions and focus. It's left efficient in remembering connections so it's good when you're making new ones. When you are open to new ideas and thinking of new things. So fuzzy brains are good for creativity. I always went to audio and walk when this happened, it worked much better.

So what about days when you're ill?

Don't learn anything new, try to revise something. At least listen to the Qur'ān, it is a healing.

Now let's speak more about the bad times a little more…

THE HARDEST CLIMBS YEALD THE MOST REWARD

"We all have problems. The way we solve them is what makes us different."

***

Believe it or not, there were two people who said that I shouldn't memorise the Qur'ān at all.

I was around 14 or 15 when a respected and well known Imām in Manchester said, "There's no point in doing Ḥifẓ. Especially anyone born and living here (UK)."

If you are reasonable, you would be shocked at such a statement. I was with my father in his office and so we asked him why. His response: "You should not memorise because in the UK anyone who memorises forgets it."

I remember my dad was fuming. The Imāms reasons were to do with those who memorise and then get busy with life's many pursuits – they end up forgetting it. His reasons were in my opinion at the time lacklustre, emotional and egotistical. It's true that there will be some people like that but there are so many that are not. Even then, you have to understand why they would forget. There are many reasons above and beyond mindset.

The other occasion someone directed a similar statement at me was when I had memorised half of the Qur'ān.

During a two year period (and a year before it) I had so many instances where I wanted to give up.

I had so many self-doubts and fears of failure. The teacher as you know did not help. He'd be strict, harsh and forceful – to the point that he'd refuse to even talk to you. He was the one who took it upon himself to say "Mubashir will never memorise the Qur'ān – he will fail" when he heard I had left for Cairo.

To this day, I don't know the truth of that statement because it is hearsay. I understood it to be emotional and possible for him to have said those words. What did I do? I simply carried on.

What people do not realise is what many people go through in order complete memorisation. Hopefully some of the following will help you during the bad times.

DEALING WITH THE BAD FELLAS, THE BAD TIMES, THE SELF-DOUBTS AND THE FEARS

1. DON'T FORGET THAT IT'S NORMAL – TALK TO OTHERS

Remind yourself that you're feeling what most other people experience. Self-doubt and fear are normal feelings. It will happen, but it should make you stronger. When I felt like that, I recognised this fact and made sure it didn't play a big factor on my memorisation. Once I recognised this I mentioned how I felt to others close to me – they'll give you a much-needed boost.

2. EMBRACE FEAR

For me, fear itself became the indicator of the things I needed to and must do – and that have had the greatest results. By doing so, you will see your confidence grow. Think about the times when you have had to make a call you were most scared of. It doesn't matter what happens, but you will walk away inspired. It is far better done than spoken. Do not be afraid of not being able to memorise or not being able to do as you wanted. The pathways are always created for you and Allāh is the best of planners.

3. GO BEYOND YOUR COMFORT ZONES

The successful Ḥāfiẓ doesn't seek comfort. He or she seeks success and are willing to do what is most uncomfortable. Most of the world today seeks comforts and familiarities: traps that cause you to settle for the mediocre. If you want to get to the next level, you've got to be comfortable being uncomfortable.

4. ASK YOURSELF: ARE MY GOALS SINCERE AND TRUE? AM I FOCUSED?

We do everything for a reason. Our goals are what drive us. If it's something you know you have to do or want to do so much, then that's one aspect of doubt you can put to rest. If not, you have some more thinking to do. Your memorisation is for your hereafter. It is for Allāh and His Messenger (peace and blessings of Allāh be upon him, his family, his companions and those who followed). Remind yourself of this fact. Remain focused.

5. LEARN FROM OTHERS

When I heard such comments it didn't affect me. It was the bad days that got to me instead. They put me in self-doubt and made me think that it wasn't for me. The way I dealt with this was to reflect on other people who had memorised the Qur'ān. I'd soon discover that the visually, audibly and mentally impaired had memorised the Qur'ān. How could I even think about stopping?

6. REMIND YOURSELF ABOUT THE REAL ENEMY

The key reminder is that shayṭān and his minions are always around (including your ego). Attempting to lure you away from recitation and memorisation. It's the last thing they want − your attachment to the Qur'ān. Realisation of this only made me stronger in my pursuits. The solution is only one: be consistent and be consistent in seeking Divine Help.

7. BAD DAYS WILL COME, TURN THEM INTO REALISATIONS

You must realise you're going to have bad times. You're going to find pain. You're going to have to climb and you're going to make sacrifices. How you deal with it depends a great deal on how you're wired. It's personal. Some prefer the pain and love to make the climb, others don't. Setbacks can be exciting but not for everyone. Once they begin to affect life around you, it becomes a real struggle. Everyone though has to deal with it.

As I mentioned before, I had the bad days. Days where I couldn't memorise, days where I kept on forgetting something, and days where I couldn't pull myself to read. Here's how I dealt with it:

- I acknowledged a bad day and got ready to change it.
- I accepted it, calmed down through remembrance and reflection. Took a break by doing something else like play or going for a walk.
- I would then review what went wrong the next day, and change it around by filling in the hole.
- Remember point 6.

8. A CALL TO PATIENCE

Do not try to rush things. Do not drop at the sight of any slip ups.

"And We will most certainly test you somewhat by means of fear and hunger and certain loss of wealth and lives and fruits. And, (O Beloved,) give glad tidings to those who observe patience." – Sūrah al-Baqarah, v.155.

9. YOU ARE NOT CHASING NUMBERS, YOU ARE CHASING QUALITY

The last thing I did was remember what was most important to me – quality time – not the quantity of time. Your aim is to memorise at the highest quality. You're committing the Words of Allāh by heart. Recognising this made making sacrifices much easier. During high school and college, I didn't go hang out with friends or take part in extra things after school/college. I would go straight home and then straight to getting ready for mosque. I would shorten my sleep, get up and learn (best time by the way). All these things and more is what counts. The Dīn calls to Iḥsān, spiritual excellence, which should be part of our daily lives. When people see amazing athletes, they forget that they practice 4-8 hours on a daily basis to be the best.

The hardest climbs yield the most reward. How much time are you prepared to do the best you can to memorise the Qur'ān?

"Make time for the Prayer, and the Prayer will make time for you."
– Abdal-Ḥakīm Murād

WHY DO IT ALONE

"Experience: that most brutal of teachers. But you learn, my God do you learn."

— C. S. Lewis.

***

My memorisation began to get a little slower. It was leading up to June quickly. I kept getting phone calls from home with my dad and everyone always asking, "how much have you memorised now?"

The pressure was mounting.

One of the key things I felt missing was the presence of somebody.

The thing is, when I was memorising in the UK I would go to class and the teacher would be present. I'd be monitored as I was memorising. This was something I was used to. In Cairo, I was faced with a different situation. I wasn't in a school. I wasn't in a Madrasah class. I was alone.

It sounds a little strange because you'd expect it would be better to be left alone. You'd get to concentrate. You can memorise more. I knew that but it can become a problem too. I was memorising in my bedroom or in the flat lounge with no one around. This is when I began to realise something. Why should I be doing it alone here when I could go to the mosque directly and study there? At home I could get distracted or become lazy.

So I was to make a new plan.

The first thing I did was to get out of the house immediately after having breakfast or lunch. I couldn't memorise in the flat any longer. I was beginning to get lazy. I've always believed in a change of environment. It's healthy. So I decided I'd go to the awesome grand mosque Masjid al-Noor. I loved that mosque. It's the mosque that holds the annual Qur'ān memorisation competitions. It has function halls, a professional library, and clean washrooms. It has comfortable clean flooring, and a great coolness inside compared to the heat in many mosques. People got married there too I think.

I started going there during the day and then go to Masjid Imām Hussain from there. From where I lived Masjid al-Noor was about 20 minutes away and Masjid Imām Hussain was about 30 minutes away. From Masjid al-Noor though, Masjid Imām Hussain was around 15 minutes away. So it meant more travelling but it also meant I was away from my flat surroundings. It worked for a while but I began to get tired of the extra travelling. It was also costing my pocket. So it made more sense to go to either Masjid al-Azhar or Masjid Imām Hussain to memorise. The Azhar mosque is one of the best in Cairo. Period. Always full of students. It felt ideal as it was near the mosque of Imām Hussain. Perfect. The only reason I dismissed it initially was because I knew there were distractions around there. Tourists and a lot more people coming in and out. So more noise, but it was worth a try.

I remember changing between both mosques. I'd go to either depending on the circumstances. What I really wanted was to go into the offices and rooms of the Imām Hussain mosque. That way I would be with and near the Imāms and teachers. Thus bringing back the element of having someone there to look over you.

One day I went to the Imām Ḥussain Masjid early.

When I got there, I found it difficult to memorise or revise. I would keep moving around the place, either someone would come near me or I would get a cat come visit me. So I started walking around which helped a little.

Suddenly Shaykh ʿAbdul Rāziq comes out. I thought I should hide or move to the back of the Masjid. He knew I was there and so he walks up to me…

"Shaykh Muḥammad!…"

By the way, my full name as Egyptians like to hear was Muḥammad Mubashir Anwar.

"…How are you?"

I respond and then he takes a seat next to me.

He says recite Sūrah Yāsīn. I don't know why but he used to say to recite that a lot of the times I saw him. At this point, I hadn't even memorised it yet. So I asked can I recite something else? He smiled and said ok.

I started reciting the last paragraph of Sūrah al-Taḥrīm (just like I mentioned before - remember the playing in my head?). After that he took a seat on a chair inside the Masjid and began talking to the guys around us. I remember him telling them that I was from Britain and came to memorise the Qur'ān. This was what I was missing in the flat. I felt the need to be around people and get some motivation. Most importantly around the teachers.

If I felt like taking it easy on travel I went to the local masjid where the teachers also knew me.

This incident highlights something. Why you shouldn't be doing your memorisation alone. The importance of teachers, mentors or anyone that can give you time and the need for them. I was in a situation where I could have carried on and on in the same fashion. Trying to memorise at home, sometimes getting really lazy or be motivated to memorise, get help and have the watchful eyes of a senior looking at you. The choice was clear. I'd speak to the Shaykh about things. We'd discuss Qira'āt, Ijazāt, Isnād, plans, and more. Shaykh never spoke much. I'd ask him questions and he'd give an insightful answer in a few words. He'd also give us food. :p

One day I went to read some of my revision.

That day there was an Indonesian brother who came to recite to him too. I went after him. I started to recite the 2nd Juz or the 5th. I was slightly affected by the fact that the guys stayed following me on their Mus'ḥaf. But it all went well until I began messing up all of a sudden so I stopped reading. I said I knew it! I don't understand what happened. The Indonesians were impressed, but I wasn't. I was still moaning. "I knew this! I don't know what is going on." (Remember I was mr perfectionist).

Shaykh then went into his other room and brought out a massive dish of warm lamb. We shared the meal. I discovered then that he had diabetes amongst other problems. May Allāh bless him.

There are many other reasons why you should find someone to do Ḥifẓ with. Amongst them mastery, error avoidance, guidance, advice, it's sunnah and much more.

The lesson: never go it alone unless you have no choice.

COMPLETION

ALWAYS BE GRATEFUL

"And He is the One Who gave you life, then He causes you to die and then will give you life again. No doubt, it is man who is highly ungrateful."
— (al-Hajj, 22:66)

"So remember Me, I shall remember you. And always be thankful to Me and never be ungrateful to Me."

— (al-Baqarah, 2:152)

***

We'll now fast forward to June.

I've still not memorised the Qur'ān yet. But my father and his three friends are about to arrive for a two-week period. Just before this I had another flatmate arrive from the UK too. Someone that my other flatmate knew. He was also a Ḥāfiẓ and a great cook. So he used to cook from now on. Thinking back, I should have taken advantage of having two Ḥuffāẓ in my apartment. But we only met in the evenings or on holidays. A signal along the journey that I missed to read perhaps.

Because my father was about to arrive and I had to finish. The plan was to let them know that I'll finish whilst they were there. So we planned a two week tour around Egypt. It was a frantic two weeks of travel back and forth for me. I got ill at one point and even one of them did too, but Shaykh 'Abdul Rāziq helped cure him. We went to Cairo and Alexandria. I didn't want them to go anywhere else apart from outskirt areas within the two week schedule. As the ultimate night was to be the night where we held the completion ceremony.

That week we went shopping. I took them to a supermarket not too different to what we'd experience in the UK. We planned to host it at the apartment of my Azhari friends - the place I stayed at when I first came to Cairo. We'd cook ourselves there. We'd call everyone we knew.

I'd be responsible for bringing Shaykh 'Abdul Rāziq and other teachers. That was possibly the most indescribable night. I hardly ate too, even though it was a celebration held in my name. That

THE PROMISE OF TEN

day I had the Azhari turban placed on my head. The night was over fast. It was time to go back to my place and my dad and company to their hotel.

The days where you memorise anything from the Qur'ān are special.

But the night you memorise the entire Qur'ān is beyond special. It's extraordinary.

With anything in life, you should be grateful. Gratitude is the base of all the successful people I've met or read about. It's the opposite of depression and anxiety. It's the conscious experience of appreciation of the gifts in our lives and the results are tangible. I learnt that night what it means to express gratitude to everyone that you can. One of the guys who came with my father was a long time friend of his. He passed away just last year. We're all going to go one day. My friend, who I spoke about before, left the world memorising when we were both aged around 15. We have to be grateful and I'm forever grateful for everything that happened after this night.

MAKES THINGS
BEAUTIFUL

"Allāh is beautiful and loves beauty."

— The Beloved Prophet
(peace and blessings of Allāh be upon him)

***

In life, we should make our experiences and creations as beautiful as possible.

My time in Cairo had to be cut short because my cousin was getting married. My plan was to remain in Cairo for another two-three months at least. I was only there for around ten months. I had to leave as the relatives wanted me there. So I left Cairo in July or August 2006.

I wasn't around in the UK for too long though, I went back to Cairo in the summer of 2007 which took my total time spent in Cairo to over a year. Whilst I was there I met a Qur'ān teacher who used to teach the guys I stayed with. He was hailed for his recitation, style and Asānīd (chains of transmission) to authorise recitation. The guys said that I had to meet him, and mentioned how he always picked out mistakes from those who recited in front of him. The day arrived.

I was introduced and so I recited. He never picked up mistakes but instead he'd always ask me to recite whenever he saw me with different requests. Sometimes he'd ask me to recite in a particular way and sometimes ask me to imitate a certain reciter.

When I started memorising the Qur'ān, I used to imitate the Imams of the Haram (which I don't recommend anyone do today). I then took to reciting more like Imām Saud Shuraim. Eventually once I opened up my 'audio range' with many reciters, I began to recite however I wanted. I began to like Mishāry Rāshid al-'Aāsy and Muḥammad Jibrīl of Egypt in particular. I would recite differently all the time and mostly dependant upon what verses I was reciting. All the while I'd always recite like

'Abdul Bāsiṭ when I was reading in public.

The Qur'ān has a natural rhyme in its structure which is often, when described, connected to poetry. And poetry is often connected to music because language, when used as poetry, has a music to it. The Qur'ān has its own unique music and recitation art form. This was one of the things I explored whilst in Cairo. I got to meet, seek advice and permissions from people like: Shaykh Aḥmad 'Āmir, Shaykh 'Abdul Rāziq, Shaykh Rabī', Shaykh Tablāwi, Dr Aḥmad Na'ayna, Shaykh Muḥammad Jibrīl and others.

Whilst in Egypt, all you would hear apart from the donkeys and car horns was the beauty of Qur'ān recitation. One thing I noticed was that everyone read in a melody whereas in England hardly anyone did (amongst students at least). Everyone just read as it were normal day to day speech in the UK.

Throughout your journey of memorisation, reciting with melody is important. In my estimation, it helps you memorise better. I noticed that time after time. Memorisation is like carving into a wall of stone. The way you carve is the way it will remain. You have to work hard to change something that you've carved into stone. It's the same with memorisation. So when you memorise - apply melody without compromising Tajwīd. Today I was talking to one of my students and said, "I know why you read so fast because you want to finish and get to play but - get serious about your Tajwīd. There is no point in memorising words when you don't read them properly, true or not true?"

***

The Beloved Prophet (peace and blessings of Allāh be upon him) said, "Beautify the Qur'ān with you voices." He also said, "Beautify your voices with the Qur'ān".

What everyone considers to be beautiful can differ. Standards also change according to times. Though we believe every voice reciting the Words of Allāh to the best level possible will all be viewed as being beautiful in the Divine Presence. From the Ḥadīth, we see that the Qur'ān beautifies voices and voices can beautify the Qur'ān. It's a two-way channel. If you think you have a bad voice, the Qur'ān will elevate it. Inherently then the Qur'ān contains beauty and any voice can encapsulate that.

The Qur'ān is a means to Allāh and we should make that means as beautiful as possible.

One of the things I was taught was that the Qur'ān is a series of love letters or letters of love. See: http://howtomemorisethequran.

com/quran-love-letter/

One of the names used to describe the Qur'ān is al-Risālah (the Message, or the Letter). If you think of the Qur'ān revelations as a series of letters from Allāh to His beloved you can begin to understand what this means. When Imām Aḥmad ibn Hanbal (may Allāh be well pleased with him) was asked "What is the best litany to read in to gain proximity with Allāh?" he said, "The recitation of the Qur'ān. The more you read it the closer you become."

Whenever someone is in love with someone they send each other letters or messages. Not only do they receive them and read them but they keep them safe, and continue to read them over and over again. If you got a letter, email, or message from someone you admired, you'd most likely treasure that letter. You'd read it a couple of times - people may even frame them. The point is that when you read these words you read them differently to an ordinary mail. There's something special about it. If you think of the Qur'ān as a series of love letters, it feels exclusive that Allāh would reveal such guidance to us. To Mankind and Jinn. Not only should you read it in a special way but you should honour it. It will change the way you approach it, recite it and understand it. As attributed to Rūmi, "Let the beauty of what you love be what you do." The aspect of beautification will make your journey enjoyable and a means of healing.

Once I noticed that a student of mine was reading a Sūrah by heart. He's never memorised them and he's never read the Qur'ān by looking completely yet. I asked him "How do you know this Sūrah?"

He said, "I didn't memorise it, I don't know how but I kind of know different Surahs." Ok great but how I asked. So he said, "My dad always has the Sūrah on the CD..."

I interrupt and say, "Aha like me then? You see I used to listen to Sūrah Rahmān and Wāqi'ah in the car when my dad used to play them. I never knew why I knew them, but I was pretty sure it was the tapes. You should tap into this as soon as you can. It's a blessing."

I also noticed he read with a tune, but he asked me how do you memorise long verses? I then pointed out that he'd already memorised a longer verse before. But I told him apart from repeating it a lot, you need to recite with a melody and you need to memorise out loud so you can hear yourself.

I can keep repeating this, but melody for me is essential.

THE JOURNEY ONLY
BEGINS NOW

A GOAL COMPLETE IS
A GOAL ONLY
JUST BEGUN

"What we call the beginning is often the end. And to make an end is to make a beginning. The end is where we start from."

— T. S. Eliot

***

To this day, I still say my memorisation journey has not finished yet.

In fact, I don't like to call myself a Ḥāfiẓ. I used to hate calling myself anything but during the last decade I've grown used to people calling me Qāri and so we rolled with that. I pray I become worthy of the title and make it a reality one day but please, don't call me Shaykh!

It's not about being humble or an alluded self-modesty. I remember, when I got back from Cairo, almost immediately I was in Scotland for the wedding. Followed by that I was in Oxfordshire for a conference. In that conference, we were joined by many scholars and artists. I was amongst the performances. During lunch on the first day after I recited one of the scholars joined me and my brother at our table. He started to ask me whether I was a Ḥāfiẓ and I said "Inshā'Allāh I hope to be". My brother then intervened and said, "He is a Ḥāfiẓ, but he's just being humble and doesn't like to say things." I was thinking, here we go, he had to do that didn't he!

The Shaykh then started to ask me further questions.

For the most part, when people ask me whether I am a Ḥāfiẓ or not I respond by saying: "Inshā'Allāh" or "I hope so" or "If Allāh accepts, yes I am". (Erm… at times, I have avoided answering the question).

The reason I do this is that I do not truly believe I am until I truly believe I have full command over the memorisation, meaning and implementation of at least one Sūrah. I've only led a few

Tarawīḥ prayers since I came back from Cairo, and for the most part I've been busy with university exams each year and so have never led them. But truth be told, I've also been avoiding them too. I am leading them this year however (2015).

When you are memorising the Qur'ān, you start a process of short term memorisation to long term memorisation. Not only that but you start something for life. Your Ḥifẓ only truly begins when you've memorised the Qur'ān. That's when the journey begins. The perceived end is the real beginning.

It is at this stage that you now have to maintain the memorisation whilst getting busier in life. You have to pass on the baton. This is where the real test begins. It's easy to memorise, but it's harder to maintain things (unless you've had a good plan implemented).

You can make it easy if you had the right process when memorising and continued this when you finished. Since I've been back in the UK, I've been busy with studies ranging from law, legal practice, Arabic, Islamic sciences of Qur'ān, Fiqh, Usul al-Fiqh, 'Aqidah, Ḥadīth, Usual al-Ḥadīth, 'Ilm al-Kalam, Tajwīd, and Tasawwuf. Connecting with teachers from the UK, Egypt, Syria, Pakistan, Uzbekistan and Australia. I've been teaching too. I've also been fortunate to do various work in different fields. Founding companies, projects and charities like How To Memorise The

Qur'ān, The Blessed Hub, The Homeless Hub and other things.

But the main thing that is always at the back of my mind is my Qur'ān.

In my room right now I have a small library of books. Ranging from Arabic texts to stories. On the top shelves, I've got my Qur'anic sciences texts. Texts written by Shaykh Khalil al-Husary, a copy of a Moroccan written Mus'ḥaf in Warsh, and a multi-narration Qur'ān I studied in Cairo. They always serve as reminders.

Many people memorise the Qur'ān and then forget it all. This is because they'd left the attachment and they haven't worked out what revision should look like and how to make it work.

I can tell you it's possible. You just have to start.

CREATE MORE MARGIN, NOT MORE GOALS

"Margin is the space between our load and our limits. It is the amount allowed beyond that which is needed."

— M.D. Richard Swenson

***

I didn't maintain revision too well when I got back during my first year at university. Here we go again.

I still wanted to make up for the time I should have been in Cairo for. As mentioned, I was in Cairo for about 10 months. I wanted to go back. So I arranged to go back in the summer of 2007. It was June and I wanted to come back for September 2007. These plans were cut short again because I had to return for August to sit exams for university.

I went along with my brother and his friend this time.

We stayed in a hotel next to the river Nile. For two weeks, they had a tour around with me like the one we did with my father. Although we also went to Luxor and planned to go to the Sinai Peninsula. They eventually left and I had to arrange a place to stay at. Who was there to help me with this? The brother that was always there for me - the Doctor - as I now call him. He gave me the keys to one of his flats in Mohandeseen which literally means engineers. Mohandessin is considered as one of the most prestigious and expensive areas of Cairo. The flat was in no way, shape, or form representative of that reputation. It was pretty poor, but it would do until I found a place. I wasn't there for too long. Even though it was close by to Imām Ḥussain mosque, I needed my own place.

Meanwhile, I look for places and eventually meet my brothers friend who was there. He arranges a place for me to stay at in Ḥayy 'āshir. It was luxury compared to what I had in Ḥayy Thāmin when I was in Nasr City in 2006, and a lot more expensive. I moved in to join a young brother from London, a professional economics dude, and a Ḥāfiẓ from the North of England. We had an interesting time together. It was due to these brothers and others that I met during my second time in Cairo that I began to document things about Ḥifẓ. It was in 2007 that I had the idea of writing a book. That book only now taking shape: "How We Memorised The Qur'ān" (http://howtomemorisethequran.com/how-we-memorised).

***

During my second trip in Cairo, I decided to ditch plan making, timetabling and any to-do listing.

I didn't do this much anyway. I always had rough estimations and plans made in my mind. But I thought if I kept breaking plans there's no point in doing things like planning. Goals are often represented in to-do lists. They can cause stress to some people. They are basically writing down everything you haven't done. And so you feel stressed out until they are complete. But they don't exactly highlight importance depending on how you do it of course.

Instead, I wanted to create an ideal week system using themes instead of goals.

My aims were to read the whole Qur'ān again during this period - even if it were 2 or 3 months. I knew that if I stuck to general themes for a day instead I will naturally do things that are important to me.

The themes are placed around 4 areas of daily practices:

1. <u>Physical</u> - sleep well, eat well, exercise.
2. <u>Emotional</u> - be around positive energy.
3. <u>Mental</u> - doing something that develops my mind.
4. <u>Spiritual</u> - taking care of the soul.

These could be translated into being creative, being healthy, less stressed and doing things that you love for the day. For instance, I'm writing this book because it's important to me. Someone asked me about how I memorised and to write it as a blog, so I promised to write it in a book instead. Writing it develops my mind, but I also get positive energy. I will then automatically do the thing that is important to me next.

Creating themes of how you want to live your life helps more than goal making and tasking I feel. It forces you to do the things that are important to you. When you create goals and lists you don't necessarily write things that are important in the moment.

You may also end up doing things that are important at a given moment. Anything random can come up. It might even be taking a nap. Goal listing can also cause disappointment when not met. Sometimes it's better to delegate things then not do anything.

To make it effective I'd have to make the themes focused into an "Ideal Week". It's like a week I could live if I could control 100 percent of what happens. Each day has a theme. Also, each day is segmented according to a specific focus area.

For example:

- **MONDAY AND TUESDAY** can be dedicated to the foundation of everything you do.
- **WEDNESDAY AND THURSDAY** can be devoted to a certain task.
- **FRIDAY** can be the day you deal strictly with other things like going out, meetings etc.
- **SATURDAY** can be for personal chores and recreation.
- **SUNDAY** can be for rest and planning.

The focus areas could be listed under timings:

- **EARLY MORNING HOURS** - for myself, reading,

praying and working out.

- **MIDDLE DAY** - for work maybe 7:30am till 6pm.
- **END OF THE DAY** - reserved for family, friends, planning.

I already had a system in place, but it was here and there. One day might have looked like this:

- **FAJR** - recite Sūrah Yāsin on most occasion, go for a walk and sleep.
- **ẒUHR** - wake up and have brunch.
- **ẒUHR TILL 'ASR** - memorise and revise.
- **'ASR** - read to the Shaykh.
- **MAGHRIB TILL 'ISHĀ** - eat my cooked dinner, chill at a local internet cafe, break.
- **AFTER 'ISHĀ** - relax at home or outside.
- **BEFORE SLEEPING** - either listening to Digital Qur'ān or reading a book.

This had to change for me to be more productive in the short time I had.

The first step and last step was to pay attention to my energy levels.

Our energy goes up and down throughout the day. Becoming aware of when you have a lot of energy and when you don't will allow you to make smarter decisions about how to structure your day. Some people do their most creative, high-value work early in the morning while others are at their best late at night. Like your energy during the day, your energy rises and falls during the week and during the year. Understanding and planning for them can help you sustain your energy over the long term.

I pretty much-shaped things around how I used to do them when I was in Cairo before apart from having the 'Ideal Week system' in place. This helped me focus on priorities and my energy levels. What helped with motivation was meeting more and more Huffāẓ. This is one of the reasons for building the #Hifz global community (join here: http://howtomemorisethequran.com/hifdh-global-community/).

What creating more margin really means is creating more space in your life. Creating space for yourself. You can become so overburdened with things and inundated with tasks that you forget about yourself. The Ideal Week can help you clear clutter, keep focused, productive but keep the most important thing intact - you.

REVISION IS EVERYTHING

"The example of the person who knows the Qur'ān by heart is like the owner of tied camels. If he keeps them tied, he will control them, but if he releases them, they will run away."

"Keep on reciting the Qur'ān, for by Him in Whose Hand is my life, the Qur'ān runs away (is forgotten) faster than camels that are released from their lead ropes."

— The Beloved Prophet
(peace and blessings of Allāh be upon him)

***

Have you ever thought about why the Prophet (peace and blessings of Allāh be upon him) used the camel as an example?

The horse could have been used as a horse is faster than a camel? But no. The Prophet (peace and blessings of Allāh be upon him) wasn't describing a camels speed of run. One understanding is that the camel was used instead because it represents memory well.

The camel takes much more work to train as compared to a horse. Memory takes a good training, especially for the memorisation of the Qur'ān. Camels are also much more intelligent. In particular, known for excellent memory traits with many able to recall a person who treated them poorly years later. Again a good link. Camels though are also known to be lazy and slow movers. Much like us. Depending on how we behave or what mood we are in, it affects our memory. Memory muscles need development. The greatest indication here however is that the camel may not be very loyal as compared to a horse. Once you release a camel from it's lead ropes it will do as it pleases. The horse can be more loyal in nature (perhaps not every horse).

We need to be loyal with the Qur'ān once we commit to memorise. We need to be even more loyal once we've completed memorisation.

As mentioned before the journey only begins after you've memorised something. Once you've memorised you can either struggle to maintain it or find a path that allows you keep connected.

When I was in Cairo during this second period, my memorisation wasn't at its peak. I had gone back to Cairo to revise. Again, the same old problem with revision. Something I haven't touched upon yet in the book in terms of the methods I used. But you will find a common theme in my journey and that is revision is everything.

If you are memorising, do not ignore revision! If you've memorised, do not ignore revision! Memorisation doesn't mean that you're done and you now know it forever. It means you've only started.

There's an example I mentioned to my students recently that goes like this.

If you are involved in a sports game - let's say football - you have to work as a team. You cannot simply keep going forward and ignore the defence. Once you ignore the defence, you are creating problems. You are likely to lose control over the game and concede many goals. If the defence is injured likewise. When the defence is very weak it forces the rest of the team to forsake creativity and move forward. They are constantly looking backwards. When you memorise, your revision is your defence. Your new portion is your midfield and your future aim is your strike. If your defence is weak everything else will be affected. Once you are solid with the foundations of the defence you can concentrate on the midfield and strike.

Here are some things to consider to help you on your journey.

SUHBAH (COMPANIONSHIP OR ASSOCIATION)

There are three to four Ḥuffāẓ living on my street. One of them memorised the Qur'ān whilst he was young part time at a local mosque. Him and his dad have had a close relationship. Everyday without fail, he recites to his father. Many do not have the luxury of doing this and others, whilst they do, they can't get themselves to recite in front of people. This fear has to go. You could get friends, teachers, siblings or parents to listen to you. Nowadays it could be people in a network online. It's where you can have someone there who can hear your problems. Listen to your revision and push you on to it. Someone who constantly asks you, inspires you and creates a positive vibe. At the time when I was doubtful, my parents were there to help for example.

This I think is one of the most important things to consider. Get help. You shouldn't be doing this alone.

REMINDERS

Reminding yourself about your purpose. The purpose of memorising the Qur'ān being broad and central to your life. This could be through watching inspiring videos, recording a message to yourself and hearing it everyday, writing a statement that you read out - all things that keep your mind frame focused. Also reminding yourself with Ḥadīth but also that shayṭān is always around. 'Why do I not feel like revising?' 'Why do I seem not to find time for it?'

EXPERIENCE

As mentioned before, seeking out those who have memorised and gaining from their experience. There's a secret for those who succeed in life and that's those who surround themselves with not only those who are better than them but also those who have vast experience.

LOOKING FOR OTHER MEMORISERS

Talking to other memorisers can also boost you. It's more effective when you can have a Ḥifẓ buddy. This way you keep each other in check and in a sense share the struggle.

RECOGNITION OF YOUR PURPOSE AND MAKING IT SACRED

Those who achieve things are patient, persistent and consistent. Consistency is crucial. When a child really wants something, they don't only show patience but they do persist constantly. What drives them is often strong desire for something or the influence of others. Likewise when you know you want, to fulfil a certain purpose, there should be the same type of drive for it. The real problem is consistency and persistence. Another thing that drives people to do things is working to deadlines and often accelerate work at the last minute. But what do you do when memorising? What do you do when you need to revise?

I think it's about creating a *sacred space and time*. During that period you cannot and will not do anything else. You have to tell other people about it too. This can help people. Remember the ideal week and themed days.

An Egyptian that I know has a daily capped amount that he must revise. It's his daily target. He makes sure he does it even if it means he has to delay sleeping. Think about the people that try to wake up for Fajr and have issues. They try setting different alarms, they try moving the alarm across the room, and anything else. The best way they ensure that they get up is by having someone wake them up. It's the same for your revision, you need waking up.

BEING ACCOUNTABLE

As you've seen you can make plans but never stick to them. One way people deal with sticking to something is by having somebody hold them to account. For example, you say to me *"I need to start revising my Qur'ān every day. I need a routine and finish one complete reading by day X. If I don't do this I want you to hold me to account. If I don't do it by XYZ I will pay/give you XYZ. You hold me to it."*

Some people actually do this and it works.

THE THING THAT IS MOST IGNORED - THE DU'A

There are so many people who desire to memorise, speak about memorising, and speak about revision. But they don't do anything. There also those that do something but they complain. All the while they never even thought about asking Allāh. They never prayed Salāt al-Hājāt (prayer for needs) and they never sought blessings through Salawāt. If you're struggling to maintain revision or get back to re-memorising the Qur'ān (in case you've forgotten), please turn to Allāh. I pray that you are successful.

DON'T DELAY, CLAIM TODAY

You don't know how long you have left on Earth. You don't know when you have the next chance to lead a prayer or recite a page form the Mus'ḥaf. If you've forgotten a Sūrah, portion, part or everything and you want to revise - why are you delaying things? Time is short. Don't delay, claim today.

***

I recently wrote an article on revision and I share it here too in case you haven't read it. See: http://howtomemorisethequran. com/how-to-dominate-your-hifdh-revision/

WHAT IS REVISION?

Revision is not repetition. Let me repeat, revision is not repetition. Revision is mastering. Often too many people revise just because they know they have to repeat things. So they don't sort out mistakes whilst they do it. They just repeat. Revision is about removing mistakes not repeating them. If you're repeating them you're not revising, you're trying to revise. This is important because after one memorises they not only have to retain what they've memorised but aim to perfect it. Perfect it in recitation and in recollection. And eventually moving onto understanding and implementation.

So how do you revise?

THE DAILY PRAYERS & NIGHT PRAYERS

A Ḥāfiẓ or a current memorizer can make a simple plan of covering revision through prayer. Far too often everyone recites the same Suwar in prayers: the last Juz or certain portions. They don't see the opportunity they have for revision.

I remember my dad used to tell me all the time, "You should revise in your prayers, it is the best way to keep it strong."

And you know what?

He's right. I realised this really late. I never did it until the day I began to do I felt two things:

1. I felt as though I was actually praying
2. I felt an amazing sensation.

The biggest part of it? You get to know exactly how strong your Qur'ān is. I remember once being at the Jumu'ah prayer and I decided to read as much as I could in the prayers. I took my phone out and made some calculations. I love to do that for some reason.

So according to what we follow as a norm, for the five prayers there are 48 Rak'at (unit/cycle/portion) in total. We know that there are 30 Parts (Ajzā''), 114 Chapters (Suwar) and 6298 verses (āyāt) of the Qur'ān. According to the sub-continental Mus'ḥaf there are around 540 to 558 paragraphs (Ruku') with four quarters for every Juz (Rub', Nisf, Thuluth and Kāmil). The Mus'ḥaf also creates a division of seven Manzil – this according to the Sunnah of a complete reading every seven days (this is also a revision method). According to the 'Uthmāni Arab script, there is a Hizb system of division. Every Juz is spilt into two halves (two Ahzāb or groups) with each half having a quarter system. So each juz will have eight-quarter divisions called a Maqra'. Meaning each Hizb (group) is subdivided into four quarters, making 240 quarters within a group of 60 Ahzāb. According what Mus'ḥaf you use, the number of pages per Juz will differ – commonly between 18-20-30.

I use the former so I looked at the number to work out a comfortable revision routine. If there are 48 Rak'at you have to take out the Farā'id due to the congregational prayers. So that's leaving you with 31 Rak'at per day for the 5 prayers. Now the way you revise using the prayers depends on how well you know your Qur'ān in the first place. If you know things really well you can easily recite a quarter or less per Rak'ah. If you don't maybe a page per Rak'ah.

That Friday I decided to start reading a page per Rak'ah per Juz as an experiment. So for Jumu'ah there would be twelve Rak'at. So I'd do the first page from each of the first 12 Juz. This means that every day I could easily complete revision of a single page per Juz, leaving one Rak'ah to read it all together. That means you will complete an entire Qur'ān every month just through the five daily prayers. That's fairly easy?

If you can't do that do a paragraph approach or a couple of verses. Then before retiring to sleep read over it all. Then you have the option of additional prayers such as Tahajjud, Awwabin, prayer of Wudu', the mosque, and other Nawāfil. There is a lot of scope and opportunities missed. You've memorised the Qur'ān for a reason – it's time to use it.

HOW DO YOU TRACK MISTAKES?

Well, when I did it sometimes whilst on a page I noticed I had to repeat certain things several times in the Rak'ah until I got it right. At other times, I just couldn't. I had to stop there and move into the Ruku'. After the units, I'd look into my phone on the Mus'haf to see where I went wrong or on my actual Mus'haf copy and make a note of the error. Start the same portion again in the next units and carrying on to the next portion. It's up to you how you do it, but another way could be to record yourself and then listen to it afterwards maybe at night. You could even only revise in the 12 Raka'āt of the Fara'id by leading a congregational prayer having a Ḥāfiẓ behind to listen. Figuring out a system for tracking mistakes is crucial.

7-8 PAGES DAILY + LISTENING = THE 90 DAY PLAN

This is a method that many people adopt but it can vary. So for every three months you'd complete a Qur'ān. If consistent of course. You'd turn out four complete readings every year.

<u>What do you do is you're alone?</u>

You first listen to the Juz throughout the day or you listen to the Juz when you're going to revise. After listening and following it's your turn. You repeat the Juz from memory but you record yourself. The next day you listen to the recording throughout the day to re-enforce it. All the while you need to track your mistakes. The next revision session arrives, now you listen to the next Juz. Repeat the process.

Of course, you can do it any way you like. You cut out the listening and record yourself and only listen to that, but the advantage of listening to a proficient reciter has more benefit. If you have someone who can listen to you then you don't have to record yourself. They can listen and mark your mistakes.

What if I know all my Qur'ān well but I have certain portions that are tough and weaker than others?

Listening to the tougher parts works. In fact listening to them more than you recite them. When you listen to something frequently, it's absorbed by parts of your brain linked to memory, and it's a very fast and effective way of memorising.

BULK REVISION AT FAJR OR AFTER

This is another popular method. People use the free time they have in the early hours for revision and so they don't need to think about it throughout the day. It's bulk for a reason. Get much as much revision as you can done but the revision has to be qualitative. It doesn't matter how much you do as an exact figure. You just keep going within a certain time frame. You could revise a quarter, a half, a Juz, two, three or five Ajzā" – it doesn't matter.

ONCE A MONTH

You make a khatam once a month by revising one Juz a day. That Juz can be revised in one sitting or it can spilt into 2, 4 or 8 sessions throughout a day.

READ OUT ALOUD, POINTING AND LOOKING INSIDE AND THEN READ FROM MEMORY

This is another method I came across. It uses more senses which can help you remember something even better. By using your sense of touch (pointing), visual, and auditory senses you can a good chance of memorising better. What you do here is simple. Pick an amount you wish to memorise and start reading out aloud, not looking anywhere else, having your finger on each line and you go along. Then recite it from memory. Each time you get stuck or make a mistake that can you noted down or the one listening to you can do that.

READING 3 JUZ DAILY BY LOOKING AND ONE JUZ BY HEART

This is a very interesting method I came across only recently. It can be done before you sleep and/or after Fajr. You can even combine audio with it. You basically do 3 Juz by looking – this doesn't mean you simply read it so quick and your done. No skim reading. Read it properly. Then do one of them by heart or another by heart. Here is an example:

Day 1 – Juz 1, 2 and 3 by looking. Juz 1 by heart.

Day 2 – Juz 2, 3 and 4 by looking. Juz 2 by heart.

Day 3 – Juz 3, 4 and 5 by looking. Juz 3 by heart.

Day 4 – Juz 4, 5, and 6 by looking. Juz 4 by heart.

Day 5 – Juz 5, 6, and 7 by looking. Juz 5 by heart.

Day 6 – Juz 6, 7 and 8 by looking. Juz 6 by heart.

Day 7 – Juz 7, 8 and 9 by looking. Juz 7 by heart.

Day 8 – Juz 8, 9 and 10 by looking. Juz 8 by heart.

Day 9 – Juz 9, 10 and 11 by looking. Juz 9 by heart.

Day 10 – Juz 10, 11 and 12 by looking. Juz 10 by heart.

This is a sound method. It ensures you get a good cycle of repetition.

ONE JUZ A MONTH BY LOOKING THEN ONE BY HEART

Similar to the last but you only do one. It might look like this:

Day 1 – Juz 2 by looking. Juz 1 by heart.

Day 2 – Juz 3 by looking. Juz 2 by heart.

Day 3 – Juz 4 by looking. Juz 3 by heart.

Day 4 – Juz 5 by looking. Juz 4 by heart.

Day 5 – Juz 6 by looking. Juz 5 by heart.

Day 6 – Juz 7 by looking. Juz 6 by heart.

Day 7 – Juz 8 by looking. Juz 7 by heart.

Day 8 – Juz 9 by looking. Juz 8 by heart.

Day 9 – Juz 10 by looking. Juz 9 by heart.

Day 10 – Juz 11 by looking. Juz 10 by heart.

A PAGE A DAY PER JUZ

This is a method that I mentioned previously but it's effective for those that don't have much time. You revise a page per Juz every day. You can create various plans for this, it's very flexible. Here is an example:

Day 1 – 1st page of Juz 1-30

Day 2 – 2nd page of Juz 1-30

Day 3 – 3rd page of Juz 1-30

Day 4 – 4th page of Juz 1-30

Day 5 – 5th page of Juz 1-30

Day 6 – 6th page of Juz 1-30

Day 7 – 7th page of Juz 1-30

Day 8 – 8th page of Juz 1-30

Day 9 – 9th page of Juz 1-30

Day 10 – 10th page of Juz 1-30

and so on till day 30. You'd do a Qur'ān every month.

You can change it of course. You can do a couple of Juz a day or a couple of pages per day, for example:

Day 1 – 1st page of Juz 1-5
Day 2 – 2nd page of Juz 1-5
Day 3 – 3rd page of Juz 1-5

Or

Day 1 – 2 pages of Juz 1-5
Day 2 – next 2 pages of Juz 1-5
Day 3 – next 2 pages of Juz 1-5.

These are just some of the methods I wanted to mention. Inshā'Allāh you can share your routines with us. I hope to be sharing a lot more in the book, *"How We Memorised The Qur'ān: A Primer on Memorisation, Revision & Teaching."*

See the book here: http://howtomemorisethequran.com/how-we-memorised-the-quran/

IT DOESN'T MATTER HOW LONG IT TAKES

"If you spend too much time thinking about a thing, you'll never get it done."

— Bruce Lee

***

When people ask me how long it took me to memorise the Qur'ān, I tend to say 'depending on how you look at it - I like to say 6 months'. You might be thinking, how can it be 6 months?! You've just told a brief story that lasts over many years. Yes, it's a journey spread over a decade. It pretty much is and I still see myself as a memoriser.

So why say 6 months?!

It depends how you look at it, I prefer to use the Egyptian experience. I effectively started again in late 2006 and it was a period where I was committed to that one thing. That period was a two part 6-month plan. But if you look at the whole journey, I didn't memorise in 6 months not even close. So whilst there might be a truth to it, it isn't the whole picture. One of the things I found about saying '6 months' is that it gave motivation and inspiration to others. I knew people who wished to do it in the same time period. So you can think of this chapter as a summary of what I'd learnt. A summary about how you could memorise within 6 months or more.

This could either get repetitive or become a book within itself so I've tried to keep this very specific for you. I'd like to add at this point that it is possible to memorise within 6 months but it takes a lot to do so. The reason I named the book the way I have was to illustrate the point of this chapter - it doesn't matter how long it takes.

GET YOUR DEFINITIONS RIGHT

We spoke about intentions and the memorisation journey mindset before. That was about understanding your motives, intentions and understandings for your journey. Make sure your mindset is well set before you begin. There's also a mindset you'll need to adopt when memorising but we'll talk about that later.

CREATE THE DEFINED PLAN

Plans are something worth doing, even if I might have said there was no point in doing them. Sometimes it helps just writing something down. This is your next step. So how do you plan a 6-month journey?

First, you need to select a copy of the Qur'ān you wish to make your companion. It's important to keep using the same copy of text when you memorise. This will aid your memory with familiarity and imagery.

Second, take a look at how many pages there are in the Qur'ān (1st to 30th taking out pages with no Qur'ān text). How many pages there are per Juz and how lines there are per page. Example: 15 lines per page, 20 pages per Juz apart from 30th and 1st, and around 620 pages.

Third, calculate how many days you have to memorise within the 6-month period. You might not be able to read everyday. Use this calculation to figure out how much you will need to memorise every day you memorise in order to finish in 6-months.

Fourth, ask yourself will I have the discipline for this? Discipline is crucial! Will this be realistic for me to achieve? In order to memorise in 6-months you're talking about around 3-4 pages per day.

Fifth, I would recommend you write it down as a plan based on applying timelines to your goals. A good way to do it would be by planning it in this way:

In __6__ months from now, I dream of having completely memorised the Qur'ān and being a Ḥāfiẓ/Hafidha.

To do so I will have to do the following today: _____
To do so I will have to do the following tomorrow: _____
To do so I will have to do the following the day after tomorrow:

_____

Sixth, pen down who you will need to contact in order for them to be your teacher or regular listener. You can do it yourself but it's a lot harder and you can create further problems.

BEFORE STARTING: TEST DRIVE AND REVISE YOUR DEFINED PLAN

First, you will need to give yourself a trial period to see whether memorising in your said plan is going to be realistic. In order to that use the Qur'ān memorisation litmus test. Pick a random page from the Qur'ān (try the first page of the 30th Juz) and give yourself a minimum of 1 hour and a maximum of 2 hours to memorise as much as you can. Before you do it consider doing it at a time you feel you're most attentive and productive (morning, afternoon, night). Sit down and start memorising with the intention/mindset telling yourself that you are memorising this page permanently. If you've memorised a whole page or more well within the time-frame, it is definitely possible for you to memorise within 6-months. If you haven't it will be a struggle, I would assess how much you memorised with this test.

You can try the test again with another random page another day at another time to figure out whether you could memorise better at that time. It all depends on when you have free time. Usually the amount you can memorise in this time (memorise well) is your starting point. You should aim to memorise that exact amount when starting.

Second, let's say you did a whole page, the next thing you need to do is go back to the same page the next day and ask someone to test you. This is the second part of the test. This part of the test will show you how well you retained the page. Depending on how well you do, this will tell you whether the amount you memorised might not be good for you starting out. You might have forgotten the whole page already for example, meaning you'd have to either memorise with more repetition but more accurately - memorise half a page with more repetition in the same time period. Remember you're not only memorising but you're building. You're revising and it's not a race. It's a well paced marathon.

Third, according to how you fair you will need to revise your plan. This might mean you will need to change figures and recalculate. Note: when memorising consistently you will notice memorisation will get easier as you get a grip on familiarity, recitation and technique.

Fourth, add to the plan. When revising the plan you will now need to consider at least one-day per week where you do not memorise but revise. You will need to consider days where you will not be able to read, holidays, times etc - no one has 365 days to play about with in the plan. Calculate the amount of time you have that is free per day, the times that you are most productive in the day. For example: (a) your best period - am, (b) your good period - pm, and (c) your bad period - pm. When calculating you can figure out how you could divide memorisation between your best periods.

After all of this you should have a solid plan. You're trying to align goals to the best of your ability, not your desired ability.

GETTING STARTED

First, before starting you will need to do some elimination. That doesn't sound like starting. It is the best start. Kill the idea of managing time but cultivate how you can manage your vision, your dream and your goal. To do that you will need to eliminate things that will get in the way in a selective manner.

It's not about fitting in more and more into a day but it's about becoming more effective (doing things getting closer to your goal), rather than being efficient (doing things quickly as possible). To do this you will need to identify things that (a) will contribute to your memorisation; (b) those things that are most important and (c) those things that will not help you in your cause. If you don't do this: minor tasks can swell to consume all your available time. You will mistake activity for productivity. You'll end up jumping from one interruption to the next without getting anything done. You'll end up wasting time either through the force of habit or by imitating what you see others doing.

Look at (c) first. You can do this through three ways:

i. Ignore anything that is irrelevant or unimportant. You will save time. Less is more.

ii. Decrease your intake load - don't read things that won't help you, surf the internet on things that won't help you, no TV, entertainment or leisure apart from at least an hour for example. The objective is to show you that the time you can spend with these things can add up to hours gone down the drain. You can follow things online by asking people instead. You can use time to memorise or revise instead.

iii. Completely ignore the unimportant - follow simple guidelines like (a) ignoring any time wasters (emails, calls, meetings, events for example) or (b) batch or delegate things you need to get done to make more time for memorisation.

Second, you don't have to reveal your goals but keep it to yourself. The Messenger of Allāh (SallAllāhu 'Alyhi wa Sallam) said *"Use discretion in fulfilling your needs."* (Tabarāni)

Third, select the right environment and room that will help enhance your memorisation experience. This is important because you don't want distractions but you want a place that will help you: (1) concentrate (2) feel relaxed (3) and be more productive. The best way to do this is to make your own space. A space that you like. An interesting advice I had was to memorise in a place that was high above anything else. In the context of a house, that could mean your loft/attic or in the context of a towering building - the roof. I did that in Cairo!

Fourth, stick to the same Mus'ḥaf (copy of the Qur'ān).

Fifth, take regular breaks.

Sixth, sleep well, eat well, and drink plenty. This will help your brain function better.

Seventh, figure out your technique. As discussed, technique or the method you use to memorise will be important. This involves the senses, technique (how), use of time and supplements. Senses: figure out what your strengths are - are they visual plus audio? Or do you need more? Technique: how you memorise it. Use of time: how the time you have available is being used productively. Supplements: what are things you can do to improve memorisation.

For a 6 month plan or any plan, a standard method is as follows:

1. You have a 3 part daily structure when you

memorise. (i) New memorisation (ii) revision of the previous 1/2 weeks and (iii) revision of the back portions. You do this every day. For example, you have completed the 30th Juz and chosen to go onto the 29th where you have done half. After your new memorisation, you revise the last weeks memorisation - that could be the whole half. Then you revise the 30th Juz.

2. You memorise by repeating the words, the sentences and the page. Combining them and repeating many times. You use audio and text.

3. You set aside at least 2-4 hours for this per day.

4. As supplements: you make constant du'a and adhkār (remembrance), drink plenty water, eat brain foods, recite a lot of Salawāt, use audio, read nawāfil, motivate yourself through meeting or learning about others.

STARTING A SESSION

First, start with praise of Allāh, Salawāt on His beloved and du'a. Then, familiarise yourself with the section or portion you wish to memorise. Look at the composition, structure and positioning of things, lengths, words, revise the Tajwīd, look at rhymes, patterns in verses, understand them etc

Second, read out aloud, slowly, carefully, listen to audio, divide long verses, make it perfect in the first round (most important), and slowly increase the amount you memorise if needed.

Third, track mistakes you make in any way you can. This could be by having a marking system on the Mus'ḥaf or an index system attached to the Mus'ḥaf logging your mistakes. Concentrate on removing mistakes before moving onto new verses.

When ending a session finish as you began with praise, Salawāt and du'a.

REVISION

As you've learnt this is the most important aspect of memorising. Make sure you don't skip a day without it. Consider a revision plan whilst memorising and after memorising.

STRIKE A BALANCE

Do not go all out onto the memorisation giving disregard to other things that are important in your life.

***

All of these things and all of the chapters above add up. If you do things right (or wrong as long as you learn from them) you will without doubt be successful. But remember one thing - it doesn't matter how long it takes you.

If you have any questions on anything or feedback get in touch with me. God-willing, I reply to everyone.

MAKE YOUR LIFE WORTH TELLING. CREATE LEGACY.

While many perceive youth as a weakness, it's actually an incredible strength.

For any young person reading this book, my message is clear. Never let anyone tell you that your dream of memorising the Qur'ān is impossible. Or any dream that you hold. No matter how big or small, you can make it real. For anyone going through a restless period in life, looking to make a change but not sure how, start with an ambitious but attainable goal. I set out to memorise the Qur'ān and connect to it. Only after I realised that it was possible and how much of a difference it made in my life did I focus on enabling anyone else to have that same experience too.

The key is to think big and then take small, incremental steps forward day by day.

Start by changing the subjects of your daily conversations from the life you are living to the life you aspire to create. By speaking the language of the person you seek to become, you will soon find yourself immersed in the conversations that make you most come alive. You'll sense the energy you emit attracting similar energy from others.

Your conversations will lead to opportunities, which will become actions, which will become footprints for good. But you can't keep saying, "I'll get started tomorrow."

The world has far too many problems, and you are way too smart and capable to not help tackle them. Your time is now. As humans we are natural storytellers. We weave narrative into nearly every relationship we build and value. I realised that I needed to live a life that reflected the themes of the stories I wanted to one day tell, and when I veered off that path later on, it was time to make a change. Regardless of age or status, if you're not satisfied with the path you're on, it's time to rewrite your future. Your life should be a story you are excited to tell. within every single person there lies an extraordinary story waiting to unfold.

The Promise of Ten awaits.

May Allāh bless you and all those you love. May Allāh grant you a love of Him, His beloved and those beloved to Them. May Allāh grant us all success here and hereafter.

PS. Pray for me too.

EPILOGUE: WHERE TO GO FROM HERE?

Wait.

It's the first book I've ever written, and as you know, God-willing I'll be releasing many more. So forgive me for any of my shortcomings.

Wherever you are in your journey, I hope you have taken away something valuable from this book. I hope you can avoid making the same mistakes I made and do something great. We are lucky in many ways to be living in this age when it's possible to do many things that weren't possible over a decade ago.

Remember to value quality over quantity. Whatever you do,

it doesn't have to be like the champs of the world but it has to be high quality. You can get there by understanding the fundamentals, playing to your strengths, and being in tune with what is most important - the hereafter.

Be part of the 5% that gets it done.

I've noticed a common trait in every successful person I know of. It's something I don't see in the rest of the population, and it's what makes them successful. It's their relentless focus on delivering something. Getting it done. Along the way they always remain grateful.

Ninety-five percent happily read a book, a quote, or listen to something, maybe even take notes, but they don't measure themselves based on what they deliver. They won't change anything.

Five percent of people do. They are the doers. It's not enough for them to read a book. It only matters when they deliver something as a result. Maybe it's brainstorming ideas, testing things, or implementing something they wanted to do.

If you DO something after reading this book, then I've succeeded with something. If you don't, then I've failed. For me that's the greatest impact because something that inspires someone often leads to results.

To make this happen, I've created a completely free Facebook group called The Promise of Ten Group (https://www.facebook.com/groups/thepromiseoften/). Outside the private community we have at #Hifdh (http://www.howtomemorisethequran.com/hifdh), I want this to be a place where we can have hundreds of members sharing and discussing various things. Either from the book or other material, and help each other build on our journeys.

Type 'The Promise of Ten Group' into Facebook and join in today. Tell us one thing you actioned in the book and become part of the 5% of people who are getting things done.

DO YOU MIND HELPING?

I have put this book out there for free and asked for nothing in return. However, if you do feel like helping out, you can do so by sharing howtomemorisethequran.com/thepromiseoften with friends or on social media, or leave an Amazon review!

If sharing on social media, do so with #ThePromiseOfTen. I like to share things that add value for people I dedicate time for when they pop up, so I'll be watching this hashtag closely on Facebook, Twitter and Instagram. Take a picture of the book when you are reading and share it online.

I'd really appreciate if you were able to do that, but only do it if you feel the book has helped you out. Be it even in the smallest of ways.

Best of luck in your own journey. I'd love for you to stay in touch with me. The best ways to do so are:

- Join my email list through howtomemorisethequran.com - I read and reply to all of my emails.
- Follow me on Twitter, @memorisingquran
- Follow and like the Facebook page: http://www.facebook.com/ howtomemorisethequran

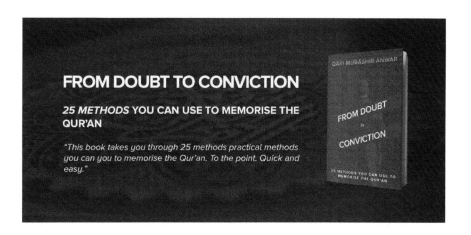

Go check it out here (it's free):
http://www.howtomemorisethequran.com/25-
methods

I'll see you on the inside!

Qāri Mubashir Anwar

ABOUT THE AUTHOR

Born and living in Manchester, UK, Qāri is a law graduate (LLB and LPC) who pursues legal, charitable, design and entrepreneurial activities. He dedicates much of his time towards various educational, social and charitable organisations/projects. He currently teaches and devises programmes pro-bono for children, teens and adults for several years. He has studied with various notable world renowned scholars from Egypt, Pakistan, Syria, Uzbekistan and Manchester.

Whilst also the founder of How To Memorise The Qur'ān, he is the author of "How We Memorised The Qur'ān: A Primer On Memorisation, Revision & Teaching" (God-willing). He is also a founder of The Blessed Hub, ImLegallyDesigned and

LawChunks amongst other initiatives. In 2011, he was recognised as being within the most highly creative 6% of the population by a market research agency.

He started memorising the Qur'ān at a very early age in his home town of Manchester, and began reciting the Holy Qur'ān to admiring audiences in public since the tender age of 10. He completed the memorisation of the Qur'ān and thus became a Hafiz in Cairo, Egypt. Whilst in Egypt he was authorised via oral permission in recitation and sought advice from various reciters. He is known for his recitation of the Qur'ān and Nashids.

GOT A QUESTION? HAVE IDEAS TO SHARE?

Leave the comment here:

http://www.howtomemorisethequran.com/contact

And you will get answers!

ACKNOWLEDGEMENTS

ALL PRAISES AND GRATITUDE BE TO ALLĀH, for giving us the ability to deliver a sound message.

AN UNLIMITED AMOUNT OF PRAYERS AND SALUTATIONS BE UPON HIS BELOVED AND OUR BELOVED MASTER - the Messenger of Allāh - through whom we got the Qur'ān and the chosen path.

SALEEM MUHAMMAD, a follower of ours and a member of #Hifdh who had constantly been messaging me about the books. I thank him for inspiring me for the idea of this book. Thanks akhi Saleem!

ANEESA TAHIR, who put up with me making her read out the first draft and make edits. And SADAF, who despite not being well read over the same draft and contributed to the editing. Thanks for the time and effort.

Thanks to my man ROJIN KHAIRUL, who the auto-type recognises as Robin. Maybe that's because he helped shape some decisions I made and proof-read the book!

Thanks to all my TEACHERS, students, seekers and followers who have inspired me to keep going in all that I do.

A special thanks to ALL OUR MEMBERS on the email lists, Facebook, and #Hifdh who have been an awesome bunch and have kept very patient with me for the release of the books. I know you're still waiting for the Primer! It will be with us soon, God willing.

Finally, THANK YOU FOR READING THE BOOK and undertaking the task of memorising the Qur'ān.

Happy memorising. :)

May Allāh bless you.

PDF VERSION

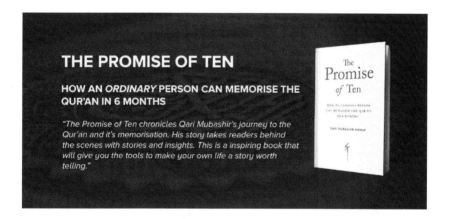

If you'd like to pick up this book in PDF format, you can download it here:

http://howtomemorisethequran.com/potdownload

FURTHER READING

Here's a list of other material that I've either written or read, you may find them helpful:

The How To Memorise The Qur'ān Blog
http://howtomemorisethequran.com/blog

Medium
https://medium.com/how-to-memorise-the-quran

Recite and Rise Up: Inspirational Ḥifẓ Stories
http://www.amazon.co.uk/Recite-Rise-Up-Inspirational-Stories-ebook/

Other material and resources
http://howtomemorisethequran.com/resources

#Hifdh The Global Community
http://howtomemorisethequran.com/hifdh

NOTES

NOTES

Printed in Great Britain
by Amazon